Powerful Places
on
The Caminos de Santiago

Gary White &
Elyn Aviva

Powerful Places on the Caminos de Santiago

by

Gary White & Elyn Aviva

ISBN: 978-0-9790909-9-8

Library of Congress Control Number:

2009944192

Set in Adobe Caslon Pro 11 pt. and Briso Pro 11 pt., with display in Adobe Caslon Pro in various sizes. Cover and title set in Reliq Std and Briso Pro

Cover photo: Santa Cristina de Lena, Pola de Lena, Asturias, by Elyn Aviva.

Contents

Acknowledgments

Gratitude to our mentors and teachers, including Ferran Blasco, Mara Freeman, Juan Li, Sig Lonegren, Anne Parker, R. J. Stewart, and Dominique Susani. Gratitude to all the earth-mystery writers and researchers, including Paul Devereux and Nigel Pennick, who have opened the way for so many others. Gratitude to each other for patience, tolerance, enthusiasm, and inspiration. Gratitude to the land, the stones, the trees, the temples. For those interested in following up with our teachers we offer the following websites:

Ferran Blasco: http://www.zahoriart.com/

Mara Freeman: http://www.chalicecentre.net/

Juan Li: http://www.ichingdao.org/tao/en/biography-of-juan-li.html

Sig Lonegren: http://www.geomancy.org/

Anne Parker: http://latitudewithattitude.com/

R. J. Stewart: http://www.rjstewart.org/

Dominique Susani: http://sacredgeometryarts.com/

Introduction

Over the years we have traveled to a number of unusual places, drawn by curiosity, lured by possibility. Gradually we realized that although many of these sites were interesting, some of them were really powerful. These were places where we felt something out of the ordinary—ranging from a shiver up the spine to an unexpected sense of serenity to a strong intimation that we had entered a "thin place" where the veil between this world and the "other realm" was more easily parted.

What we experienced in these places was an interaction between the energy of the place itself, the human activities at that location (offerings, ceremonies, constructions such as stone circles or temples), and our own openness to experience what was happening at that moment. The feeling that a particular place is powerful can take many forms, and it can be subtle or very strong.

In this guidebook we describe some of the more powerful places we have found on the various Caminos de Santiago. We make no claims as to what you may or may not feel when visiting these sites. We have observed that one person may bask in the energy of a particular site, another may feel nothing at all, and a third may want to leave as quickly as possible.

On one visit inside a large, earth-covered passage tomb in Ireland, Elyn felt increasingly uncomfortable and shaky but (against her better judgment) stayed to listen to our guide. Afterwards, Elyn took a survey and discovered that several people had left immediately because they felt so ill at ease—and others thought it was a wonderful place in which to meditate. In an isolated monastery in the mountains of Spain, Elyn and Gary were shown into an abandoned chapel. Instantly, they both felt an incredibly unconditional loving presence. Their companion (a very sensitive and intuitive lady) looked at them in puzzlement. She thought the energy in the room was nothing special.

Sometimes our experience has differed on subsequent visits to the same site. We speculate why this may be, but we realize that experiences can never be repeated—whether it's your first taste of a chocolate gelato cone on a sunny day in Rome, or your first kiss, or your first visit to the Grand Canyon. As the Greek philosopher Heraclitus said, "No man ever steps in the same river twice, for it's not the same river and he's not the same man." This is equally true of powerful places.

What makes a place powerful?

The brief answer to "what" is: the land itself has underground water lines, faults or cracks in the earth (sometimes called fire lines), energy vortices, "blind" springs, and so on that our ancestors were able to sense and utilize. An old Gaulish word, *wouivre*, refers to snakes that glide, to rivers that snake through the landscape, and to telluric currents that snake underground from the depths of the terrestrial strata. Experienced dowsers using dowsing rods or pendulums can locate these underground features with great accuracy. If they couldn't, oil exploration and well-digging companies wouldn't waste their money on hiring them.

Our ancestors utilized these energies—and their knowledge of geometry (circles, triangles, pyramid shapes, etc.)—to construct sacred places. For example, an alignment of standing stones may have been placed to draw off energy from an underground fault; a circle of stones may have been built to utilize the energy of an underground spring. The altar of a twelfth-century church may have been carefully placed over the crossing of underground water and fault or fire lines.

How do you sense these energies?

The brief answer to how to sense these energies is: by centering, grounding, and being present to a site *in whatever way works for you.* Feeling the subtle energies that are present in a place requires sensitivity and intuition. It is a bit like tuning a radio dial to a particular frequency. These techniques can be taught (we have studied with several teachers who have taught us how). Such instruction is outside the scope of this guidebook, although we do give a few suggestions for how you can be more attuned to a powerful place.

We encourage you to listen carefully to your own inner guidance as you open yourself to what may be available to you at a particular place on a particular day, at a particular time of day, with the particular predisposition you bring at that moment. You must use your own judgment about what is good or not good for you. Trust your feelings—and enjoy the mystery.

Organization

Each chapter begins with a brief account by Elyn of a visit to a particular powerful place. This is followed by information about the site along with suggestions, quotations, and related graphics. At the end of each chapter are directions on how to get there and a brief space (Notes) for you to add your own observations. The guidebook concludes with a glossary and bibliography.

How did we choose these particular locations? We talked with people; we did research in books and on the web to discover possible powerful places that were not likely to be on every tourist's itinerary; we have lived in Spain for several years and traveled extensively there; Elyn has made a life-long study of the Camino, leading to her PhD in anthropology in 1985, and written a number of books on the subject; and we paid attention to what we experienced at different sites. We then selected powerful places to include in this guidebook.

This specialized guidebook is not an exhaustive listing of all the powerful places on the Caminos de Santiago; to do that would require many volumes. Nor is it a complete guide to what to see or where to stay in Spain. For that you'll need to consult a general travel book. This guidebook is intended as an invitation to experience powerful places on the Caminos de Santiago in Spain. We hope that it's the beginning of a conversation. We'd like to hear from you.

Around the Caminos

There are many ways to go to Santiago—in fact, sometimes it seems as if "all roads lead to Santiago"—at least in Spain. For over a millennium, pilgrims have traveled across Europe to reach the shrine of St. James the Greater, the first martyred apostle, believed to be buried in Santiago de Compostela in northwestern Galicia. Depending on where they came from in Spain or elsewhere, and which shrines they chose to visit along the way, they favored certain routes over others. The Caminos de Santiago formed a complex network of roads, some Roman, some medieval, all across Spain.

The main Camino de Santiago across Spain was (and still is) known as the Camino Francés because so many French pilgrims followed it and French Cluny monks established numerous monasteries along the way. But there are other routes as well, including the Vía de la Plata that comes up from the south; the Camino de San Salvador that leads from León north to Oviedo (a recommended diversion in medieval times); the Camino del Norte that goes along the Cantabrian coast—and many others.

There are many sacred sites worth visiting on the Camino Francés—gorgeous cathedrals, intriguing Romanesque churches, isolated monasteries. Some claim that the entire Camino de Santiago (a.k.a. the Camino Francés) is itself a powerful place that follows the path of the Milky Way across the night sky—an alchemical journey that leads to deep personal transformation. A number of books describe this pilgrimage road (and even the esoteric journey) in detail. For that reason

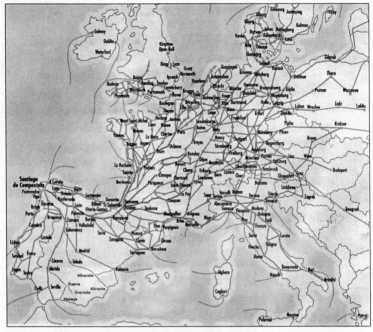

The Caminos de Santiago

we have selected some of the most powerful places on some of the less-well-known Caminos de Santiago to include in this guidebook.

A number of these alternative Caminos are currently being reclaimed: they are marked with painted yellow arrows and more sophisticated signage supplied by the European Union. Road signs often point the way for those wanting to diverge from the main Camino Francés and take a road less traveled. Albergues and pilgrimage refuges are being established to meet the needs of the ever-increasing number of pilgrims following these alternative routes.

10. San Andrés de Teixido

11. Fisterre
9. Santa Cristina de Lena
2. Valle de Hecho
4. Monastery of Leyre
3. San Juan de la Peña
5. San Millán de la Cogolla
8. Quintanilla de las Viñas
7. San Bartolomé, Canyon de Rio Lobos
6. San Baudelio de Berlanaga
1. Monserrat

Northern Spain

Powerful places in this book

Today, as in the Middle Ages, people travel to Santiago for many reasons, ranging from deep religious faith to adventure, from spiritual quest to outdoor enthusiasm. But unless you are a truly dedicated pilgrim and a serious walker, you will probably prefer to travel by car to reach the powerful places we describe in this guidebook. If you decide to drive we highly recommend that you purchase a detailed road atlas and/or use a GPS device.

You will note that sometimes we provide alternative spellings for place names. Spain has several regional languages, including Gallego in Galicia and Catalan in Catalunya (Catalonia). We give these regional languages priority but also provide the Castilian ("Spanish") place names as alternatives.

Experiencing a Powerful Place

This is a guidebook about *experiencing* places—not just seeing them. You may have already developed your own way to visit a powerful place. If not, the following may be of use.

Much of the time we humans operate on "automatic," hardly registering where we are or what we feel. Visiting a powerful place is an opportunity to be intentional and alert. In order to fully experience a powerful place, it is important to be present. Really conscious. Really aware of your surroundings and of changes in yourself in response to your surroundings. We suggest an acronym, **BLESSING**, to help remember how to prepare to enter a powerful place—whether it is a forest, a church, or a stone circle.

BLESSING stands for: **B**reathe slowly and regularly, paying attention to your breath moving in and out. If you have a breathing practice, now is the time to do it. **L**ook and **L**isten within: what are you sensing internally? How do you feel? **E**stablish yourself in your location, perhaps by orienting to the seven directions (east, south, west, north, above, below, and the center within—or, before you, behind you, to your right, to your left, above, below, and the center within). **S**ense your surroundings, opening up your five senses (and sixth sense) to

Going to a powerful place is like getting to know a new friend. Don't rush in. Say "hello." Introduce yourself. Bring a "hostess" gift. Listen politely to what the site has to tell you. Don't be rude or impatient. Don't interrupt. Have a conversation. When you (and it) are finished, don't just leave—remember to say goodbye. And realize that not every powerful place wants to be befriended! Some might be positively taciturn or even grumpy.

what is around you. State your **IN**tention to respect this place, to experience what is present. **G**ive gratitude for this opportunity.

In approaching a powerful place, it is very important that we prepare ourselves mentally, emotionally, psychologically, and physically for the experience because what we feel is very much determined by what we bring to the site. Purposeful preparation becomes the prerequisite for having meaningful experiences.

One of our mentors, Mara Freeman, suggests the acronym **ECOLOGY** for remembering how to approach a stone circle. It can, of course, be modified to apply to powerful places in general. "E" stands for **E**ntry, which means enter by first circling the site in a clockwise (sunwise) direction. "C" is for **C**entering yourself. This is often best accomplished by touching one of the stones. "O" stands for **O**ffering, which can be a bit of grain, milk, a strand of hair, saliva, etc., which shows that you come in good faith. The best offerings are biodegradable so they don't linger in the environment to build up over time. "L" is for **L**istening—listen to the sounds around you: birds, wind, wild creatures, and other sounds of nature. "O" stands for **O**pening up your inner and outer senses. "G" is for **G**ratitude to the place, the Earth, all of life, and Nature. "Y" is for **Y**ou: you should leave a place just as you found it. Take nothing and leave nothing. You can see the result of people not observing this injunction at many popular sacred sites: trees damaged by people taking pieces of their bark or carving on them; sites littered with paper wrappers and trash; melted wax dripped over ancient stones. Observe **ECOLOGY**: the Earth and future visitors will thank you.

Elyn Aviva

Holy cave at Montserrat

Montserrat, Catalunya

I saw the mountain range rise abruptly out of the plains, shocking and jagged like a sharp-toothed saw blade. Montserrat. Home of "La Moreneta," the Black Virgin who is patroness of Catalonia. Her shrine has been visited for over 800 years by pilgrims on their way from the east to Santiago. A trail sign—Camí Sant Jaume—points the way.

The road to her sanctuary twists and climbs tortuously up the side of the mountain. Traffic was heavy, waiting long, expectation growing. We arrived at last and walked down the trail that winds across the mountain to the Holy Cave where an image of the Virgin was found. The scent of incense suddenly filled the air: presence of the Divine?

The next morning we visited "La Moreneta" in her glittering, mosaic-filled chamber high above the nave of the basilica. We arrived early and stayed long, the melodious sound of Lauds wafting up to where we stood in grateful prayer. Her right hand, holding a globe, reaches out through an opening in the glass case that surrounds her. I touched it, thrilled to be so intimate. In her presence I sensed compassion and peace, and endless patience. Dark, silent, still, she hints at—points to—something beyond form. (Elyn)

A guidebook for Montserrat asks the question, "What is Montserrat?" and answers with "a mountain, a sanctuary, a monastery, a spiritual community." Montserrat is all of these and more, including the oldest continuously operating publishing company in the world. Its first book was printed over 500 years ago. The mountain itself, with its towering crags carved by

12

wind and rain from a conglomerate stone of yellow-pink color, dominates the horizon for many miles around. You can ascend the mountain in several ways. The fastest is by cable car, but the cog railway or the

Montserrat

highway will give you more of an appreciation for the isolation of this airy perch.

Montserrat is not on the way to anywhere else (except, perhaps, Santiago de Compostela), so the hundreds of thousands of pilgrims and tourists who ascend the mountain each year are going there to ap-

Elyn Aviva

"La Moreneta"

preciate the sanctuary, the monastery, the spiritual community, or the boys' choir—if they are not simply checking off another sight from their list of places to see.

When approaching the monastery complex you are likely to be put off by the bus- and train-loads of tourists who fill the plazas and shops, but don't be discouraged—the sanctuary is really worth the effort. We recommend that you stay the night in the hotel near the sanctuary (Google Hotel Abat Cisneros). In the evening and early morning you will have the place nearly to yourself and the true spirit of Montserrat will emerge.

The Holy Cave (Santa Cova)

Legend has it that the image of Our Lady of Montserrat in the basilica was found in a small cave on a cliff about a mile from the sanctuary. The path to the cave, which is sheltered inside a stone chapel, begins near the cable-car station. The walk is not difficult though the first part of it descends steeply. Along the way you can admire the sculptural groups by several famous artists depicting the fifteen Mysteries of the Rosary. Inside the chapel a modern sculpture of Our Lady of Montserrat is venerated in one room. Another room is filled with ex votos left by people who came to Montserrat for healing. The place is peaceful and quiet. We found a sweet

"Spokesmen for the Church, when asked to explain the origin of Black Virgins, tend to invoke candle smoke or general exposure to the elements. After a time, they would say, as at Einsiedeln, the faithful become accustomed to a sooty image, and the clergy pander to their prejudice by the use of paint where necessary. Apart from the considerable contrary evidence of clerical antipathy to Black Virgins and disregard for parishioners' wishes, this rationalistic hypothesis raises two important questions. If the presumed polychrome faces and hands of the Virgin and Child have been blackened by the elements, why has their polychrome clothing not been similarly discoloured? Secondly, why has a similar process not occurred in the case of other venerated images?" Ean Begg. *The Cult of the Black Virgin*. Revised and expanded edition. London: Penguin Books, 1985, p. 6.

14

and placid energy there that amply rewarded our hike. (After walking two-thirds of the way back, we rode the funicular up the steepest incline.)

The Atrium before the Basilica

Enter through the center of the five archways in the front of the Benedictine monastery and you will find yourself in a square atrium with an elaborate mandala laid in stone in the pavement. You may see people standing in the center with arms raised. That's because the exact center, which is marked by a round medallion, is known as a "power place." Stand in the center of the medallion and see what you feel. There is a second medallion at the entrance to the atrium, and if one person stands there it is said that the energy in the center increases many-fold. We visited the atrium at night when there were few other people and felt significant energy at this point.

Elyn Aviva

The mandala in the atrium

The Basilica

There are two main entrances to the basilica. The one on the right of the atrium leads to the chapel of Our Lady of Montserrat, located above and behind the main altar. The door in the center leads to the nave of the church. The basilica is a reconstructed sixteenth-century Gothic/Renaissance design with unusual rounded arches, which harken back to the Romanesque. It is elaborately decorated throughout and quite impressive. Try to visit when the famed Montserrat Boys' Choir is performing the *Salve Regina* at mid-day. They are often joined by the monastic choir and the resulting musical experience is outstanding.

"La Moreneta"

During the day, tourists and pilgrims wait patiently in line for a few moments before the image of "La Moreneta," which resides in a tiny chapel one floor above the nave of the basilica. One advantage to staying overnight on the mountain is that the door to Our Lady's chapel opens early (around 7:00 or 7:30 AM), well before the hoards of tourists arrive. You may be able to have her nearly to yourself at that time. We found the chapel filled with a powerful, loving energy and were able to linger there for many minutes while the monks chanted Lauds below in the basilica. What a wonderful way to begin the day. We strolled back to our hotel for breakfast still aware of "La Moreneta's" calm, sweet energy, which

"Regardless of the party line that attempts to rationalize away the significance of her blackness, her devotees know that Black Madonnas have a lot of miracle-making juju. Feminist scholars and Jungian psychologists hypothesize this is because the Black Madonna represents the chthonic forces of the Earth, the cave, the darkness of the soil from which seeds sprout, the recuperative powers of night or sleep, and the shadow." Elyn Aviva. *Walking Through Cancer: A Pilgrimage of Gratitude on the Way of St. James.* Santa Fe: Pilgrims Process, Inc., 2009, p. 47-48.

lingered for hours as we visited the shops, museums, and other sites on the mountain.

Other Things to Do

Montserrat offers many other opportunities for those who can stay for a few days. The museum con-

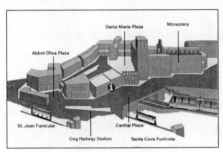

Some Montserrat landmarks

tains a collection of paintings by "old masters" along with works by many twentieth-century Catalan artists. There is a *Via Crucis* (Stations of the Cross), trails leading to the remains of ancient hermitages, and a funicular ride to the top of the mountain, which offers spectacular views. Many Catalans make an annual visit to Montserrat for cultural events that take place there. Go online to http://www.sacred-destinations.com/spain/montserrat-shrine.htm   to find out more.

Getting There

Many package tours that include Montserrat are available from Barcelona. Remember when you Google for tours to put in "Tours to Montserrat, Spain" to avoid tours to the island of Montserrat. Some packages include tours to the surrounding wine country; guided as well as self-guided tours are available. An interesting self-guided option is a package offered by the cog railway company that includes a

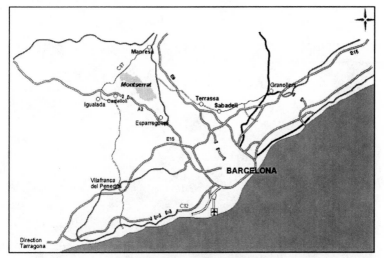

From Barcelona to Montserrat

combination of train, cog railway, and funicular travel to and from the mountain. See their website at www. cremallerademontserrat.cat for details.

If you are driving, be prepared for some very narrow and steep mountain roads. Delays are common since there is a gate at the top that only admits a car when there is space for it to park in the limited parking lot on top of the mountain. In busy times this can amount to several hours of delay, so we don't recommend driving up to Montserrat, especially on weekends or holidays.

Notes

Aguas Tuertas

Valle de Hecho (San Pedro de Siresa; Aguas Tuertas), Huesca Province, Aragón

The Valley of Echo: A narrow Pyrenean valley with a river running through, abundant hiking trails, towering mountains, deep forests—and isolated, ancient sanctuaries more easily reached by birds than humans. We walked part of the Roman road that pilgrims followed a millennium ago on their way to Santiago. Later, in Siresa, we entered the Church of San Pedro. It is nearly bare, long robbed of finery and fluff, but the bare bones of stones know their stuff and fill the space with sweet resonance. I walked the cobblestone spiral in the nave, pondering its twisting turns, tightening like a spring....

The next day, a journey high into the mountains, past the Roman road and turning right. The car can go no further so we walk, scrambling along the sides of hills until at last rejoining the gravel track. Suddenly, the path leads abruptly down and before us is Shangri La: a high mountain valley, flat, wide, and green. Horses gallop across the gentle bends in the twisting stream, shaking their manes and pawing at the grass. The light is golden, preternaturally clear. "Nature is the true temple," and we have stumbled on the holy grail. (Elyn)

The Valle de Echo (Valley of Hecho) contains one of several paths over the Pyrenees that medieval pilgrims, merchants, and other travelers followed to enter Spain. Local legend says that the Roman road from the pass at Puerto de Palo is the original Camino de Santiago, predating the road from San Jean Pied de Port to Roncesvalles and the road through

20

Elyn Aviva

Somport Pass. Whether it is the "first" camino or not, it is certainly a route that dates from earlier times. The Roman road (Via Romana) over the pass can still be walked today. The way is clearly marked where it crosses the HU-V-2131 highway north of Siresa and can be followed all the way through the Puerto de Palo and into France.

The first part of this trail is an easy walk and gives one a good impression of what a Roman road might have been like, but the latter part up to the Puerto de Palo is arduous and should only be attempted by seasoned hikers. For us, the power of this walk comes from knowing that you are walking a road that is little changed from Roman

Elyn Aviva

Gary on the Roman road

times. Those who are sensitive to past-life experiences may find much to contemplate while walking this road. We certainly felt the presence of those who had followed this route a millennium or two ago.

Church of the Monastery of San Pedro

If this road *is* the original Camino de Santiago, then the Monastery of San Pedro in Siresa would have been the pilgrims' first stop in Spain on their way to Santiago. The monastery was founded in 833 CE; the present church, dating from the eleventh century, is one of the oldest Romanesque buildings in Spain.

Church of the Monastery of San Pedro

This imposing structure dominates the small town of Siresa and bespeaks a time when Siresa was an important political and religious center. The central nave is dominated by a spiral pattern laid in the cobblestones of the floor, which gives the space a lively energy. Walk it and see if you notice changes in the atmosphere of the church.

St. Peter

An impressive statue of a scowling St. Peter sits behind the altar. The Apostle wears a three-level hat and three-level brooch (referring to lower, middle, and upper realms?) and holds the keys to the kingdom. He also clasps a closed book. Don't miss the Gothic *retablo* of St. James the Greater in the north crossing. The *retablo* is also divided into three levels.

The Benedictine monastery in Siresa was an early center of learning. By the late ninth century it housed an extensive collection of manuscripts, including works by Virgil, Horace, Juvenal, Porphyry, Aldhelm, and Augustine of Hippo. Alfonso el Batallador, King of Aragon in the twelfth century, received his education at the monastery.

Aguas Tuertas

If you drive north of the town of Siresa to the end of the narrow paved road (drive on past the campgrounds) you will find a gravel road that turns into a track and leads up sharply to the high alpine meadow of Aguas Tuertas (Twisted Waters). (http://www.summitpost.org/route/160332/valle-de-aguas-tuertas.html) The track up to the meadow is somewhat challenging, but the valley above is well worth the effort. Along the way you will encounter a megalithic site

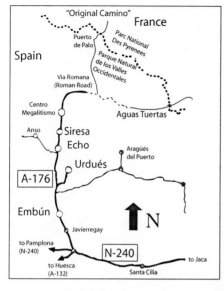

called the Tumulus of Salto, a prehistoric passage "tomb" covered with stones. (Although called a tomb, it was probably much more— perhaps related to undergound energies.) A spectacular double waterfall tumbles down just before the steepest part of the climb up to the valley. Out of sight behind the waterfall is the large meadow. A small creek (Aguas Tuertas) snakes back and forth across the valley. There are several dolmens in the valley.

For us, the valley was the most idyllic place in the Valle de Echo. We bathed in the stream; watched shepherds on foot herding a large herd of horses, some with young colts; and ate our lunch sitting on the lush green grass at the edge of the creek. In this valley we discovered again that the most powerful temples are the temples of nature. We returned to the lower slopes refreshed and grateful for the beauty we had witnessed.

> "Nature is the true temple."
> Ferran Blasco

Getting There

Drive on the N-240 east from Pamplona or west from Jaca. Near Puente la Reina take A-176 north to

Hecho (Echo). North of Hecho (Echo) take HU-V-2131 north to Siresa. At the time of our writing this, a new high-speed motorway is under construction from Pamplona to Jaca. When this highway is completed it may affect the intersection with A-176.

Getting to Aguas Tuertas depends on the vehicle you are driving and your taste for walking. You can park at the end of the paved road or drive on gravel to the Plano do Mallo. There are information signs at that point. If you have a four-wheel drive vehicle and don't want to walk far, you might attempt driving further along the gravel track. We recommend picking up a detailed topographical map and hiking guide for the Parque Natural de los Valles Occidentales, which is available in Siresa or Echo. The guide we purchased was the *Guía Excursionista for Ansó-Echo, Aragües-Jasa,* published by the Federación Aragonesa de Montañismo.

Notes

Cloister, San Juan de la Peña

San Juan de la Peña and Santa María de Serós, Huesca Province, Aragón

San Juan de la Peña didn't look real at first, its delicate cloister sheltered beneath a bulging overhang of rock, high above the road. We entered below, into the original building constructed a millennium ago around the caves of hermits. A moss-covered spring trickled from the rock wall, its water dripping down into the floor below. For centuries, monks had lived and prayed here, imbuing the very atmosphere with sacredness.... Seven steps lead to the chapel: seven chakras, climbing up to Spirit? "They" say that the Holy Grail was hidden here. A replica is on display, looking like a stage prop inadvertently left behind. The cloister is breath-taking. (Elyn)

The early history of the monastery at San Juan de la Peña is unknown, but it is clear that it developed out of a hermit's cave at the present site. The first documentary evidence of the monastery comes from the tenth century, by which time the monastery was already well established and the monks were ministering to the needs of pilgrims on their way to Santiago de Compostela. The lower level of the building may have been the monks' dormitory, which includes a spring that issues from the bare rock. There is a small chapel in the next room. We experienced considerable energy in this pre-Romanesque chapel

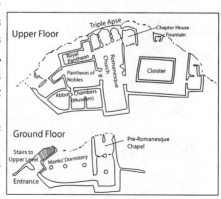

Floor plan of San Juan de la Peña

28

once we activated it by walking sunwise around the room and standing in the four corners.

It is in the upper level of the building that the later history of San Juan de la Peña unfolds. San Juan is the burial place for the kings of Aragón; a pantheon memorializes lesser nobles. The Romanesque church has a triple apse, and a replica of a replica of the so-called Holy Grail is displayed on an altar in the central apse.

Activating the pre-Romanesque chapel

Elyn Aviva

Perhaps some of the power we felt in this holy location *is* associated with the mystery of the Holy Grail.

The replica of the Holy Grail

Whether the Grail is an actual physical object—and what the nature of that object might be—is the subject of much speculation. In San Juan de la Peña the Holy Grail is believed to be a cup that now resides in the cathedral in Valencia. Others claim that the Grail is in Genoa, Glastonbury, Rosslyn Chapel in Scotland, Oak Island in Nova Scotia, and even

"Another story, probably apocryphal, describes how the original Cup of the Last Supper was hidden in the cave of San Juan de la Peña in 713 (though it is not suggested how it came there) by an Aragonese Bishop named Audebert. When Aragón was threatened by the Moors at the beginning of the twelfth century, the sacred Cup was removed and taken to the Pyrenees, where it was entrusted to the Cathars. When they were destroyed, the Cup was smuggled back into Spain and hidden in the cave again, this time under the protection of Don Martín L'Humain, the then King of Aragón. In later years the Cup was identified with one kept in the Cathedral of Valencia, but which had now further acquired the identification with the vessel given to Solomon by the Queen of Sheba. Wildly improbable though this story may seem at first glance there is a ring of authenticity about it. Nor should one overlook the fact that it is to the Cathars that the precious object is entrusted." John Matthews. *The Elements of the Grail Tradition.* Shaftesbury, Dorset: Element Books Limited. 1990, p. 63.

in a small abbey in the upper Midwest of the United States. Rudolph Steiner claimed that the chalice in Valencia originally came to San Juan de la Peña from the monastery of Suso (see page 44). Needless to say, it is impossible to verify the truth of any of these assertions. But perhaps there is some truth there nevertheless.

What you also won't learn in the abbot's quarters/museum on the upper floor are the details of centuries of political/religious infighting, various law suits over financial matters, and several fires, which left the monastery unfit for habitation in the mid-seventeenth century. A new monastery was then constructed one mile up the road. That building now houses a hotel and restaurant complex, along with an interpretative center for San Juan de la Peña and the Kingdom of Aragón. (Google Hospederia Monasterio San Juan de la Peña)

The old monastery was never totally abandoned because it contained royal remains. Various attempts at restoration were made until, in the mid-nineteenth century, the Spanish government sold it as a part of the "disentailment," a process of confiscation of church property aimed at bringing more land under

The cloister in 1844

taxation. It lay in ruins for years before it was declared a National Monument in 1889. Various attempts at restoration ensued, most of which were later removed, making way for the latest restoration in the 1980s.

The Cloister

The Romanesque church, the Pantheon of the Nobles, and the museum are all worth a visit, but it is the pre-Romanesque church and the twelfth-century cloister that make San Juan a powerful place in our estimation. Located on a terrace outside the church and protected from the ele-

"In addition to modifying antique forms, Romanesque sculptors invented new forms of representation of their own. Their use of capitals as a field for decorative and figurative illustration is a prime example. Decorated capitals are most often found in the crypts of churches, high above the sanctuary, along the nave, and, most importantly, in the cloister." Andreas Petzold. *Romanesque Art*. Upper Saddle River, NJ: Prentice Hall, 1995, p. 53.

ments by the overhanging rock, the cloister is a masterpiece of perfect proportions. Try walking around the outside of the cloister three times clockwise (sunwise) to raise the energy of the space and see what you feel.

The capitals on the surviving columns of the cloister are beautifully preserved. Here you will see the story of Genesis from the creation of Adam and Eve through their expulsion from the Garden of Eden, the Annunciation, scenes from the life of Christ, along with various fanciful animals and birds. You might find alchemical references as well, such as an open and closed oven.

The Convent of Santa María de la Serós

On the road to (or from) San Juan de la Peña, stop in the little town of Santa Cruz de la Serós to have lunch and spend some time at the remains of the convent that was the sister house of San Juan de la Peña.

All that is left of the Convent of Santa María de la Serós is the impressive church and attached tower. Santa María de la Serós was an important convent during the early history of San Juan de la Peña. Daughters and widows of noble families lodged in the community, and

The church of Santa María

the convent enjoyed similar royal privileges to those of the monastery. The convent achieved peak importance during the eleventh century and remained active until 1555, when the nuns moved to Jaca.

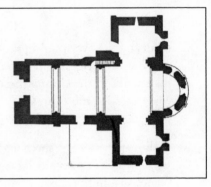

Floor plan of Santa María

The Church of Santa María is a Latin cross with a single nave. The interior is austere but imbued with a pure, sweet energy. The side chapels contain Renaissance retablos of considerable interest. Until recently it was possible to ascend the spiral staircase to the tower into the intriguing octagonal room above, but this is now closed due to an unfortunate accident.

Other Things to Do

The monastery is located in the Monumento Natural de San Juan de la Peña, which offers signposted nature walks and hiking

A fanciful 1724 drawing of the new and old monasteries of San Juan de la Peña

trails in beautiful wilderness surroundings. We recommend that you purchase a topographical map of the area if you are interested in these offerings. The guide we purchased at the San Juan de la Peña ticket office is the *Guía Excursionista for Monumento Natural de San Juan de la Peña,* published by the Federación Aragonesa de Montañismo.

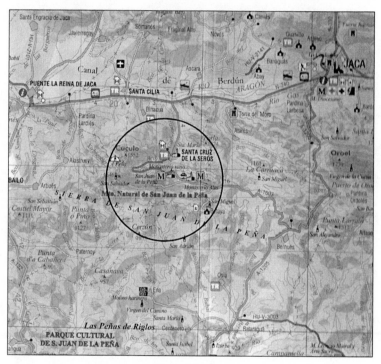

Map of the area

Getting There

Drive the N-240 east from Puente La Reina de Jaca or west from Jaca. At about the halfway point between these two towns take the HU-V-2301 south to Santa

Cruz de la Serós. From there the road continues four miles to San Juan de la Peña. You will probably not be able to park near the old monastery. If so, continue up the hill to the upper (new) monastery where there is ample parking, a campground, and a hotel/restaurant. From the new monastery you can walk down to the old monastery on a signposted nature trail.

A shuttle bus is also available to and from the monastery. When we were last there, we walked down and took the bus back to the upper parking lot, thus enjoying the advantage of the nature walk without having a steep climb on the return.

To enter the old monastery you will need to purchase a ticket in the booth located across the road from it.

The camping area or the hotel would both be possible choices if you want to extend your stay and enjoy the wilderness areas. The restaurant/hostal next to Santa María de la Serós in Santa Cruz de la Serós offers excellent regional specialties, including wild boar stew.

Notes

Elyn Aviva

The crypt of the Monastery of Leyre

Monasterio de Leyre, Navarra Province

The crypt is weirdly beautiful, its low arches ending at waist height with strangely carved capitals. On one, spirals resolve into what look like wings. Or maybe the Eye of Horus, though how Egypt got here is a mystery. On another, twin spirals face away from each other but join in a single stem that then fans out into four. What do they represent? An ovary on either side of the birth canal? A tree of life? A horned beast? No matter. I am perplexed. I feel the weight of the church above, pressing down on the stubby columns.

In the church above (directly above the crypt, in fact), the Virgin of Leyre sits on her throne, spreading compassion and love throughout her realm. I'm sure the monks feel it when they come to chant the daily round of offices. We hear them one evening, and I see the Virgin watch approvingly, like a proud mother. (Elyn)

The Monastery of San Salvador in Leyre has a history that is, in many ways, similar to the history of many other Spanish monasteries. After being established in the first half of the ninth century and rising to prominence in later centuries, it fell into decline and was abandoned in the nineteenth century during the confiscation of church property by the government (the disentailment). The property was restored in the twentieth century by the Navarre Regional Government.

Leyre in ruins in the nineteenth century

Benedictine monks from Santo Domingo de Silos arrived in 1954 to renew monastic life in Leyre.

The monastery is active today and has become a popular vacation retreat (www.monasteriodeleyre. com). The oldest section of the monastery has been turned into a hotel/restaurant (www.hotelhospederiadeleyre.com). The monks maintain their monastic life with regular times of worship, and they are well known for their inspiring singing of Gregorian chant; you can attend services in the church.

The monastery lies in the foothills of the Sierra de Erando and enjoys a sweeping view of mountains and

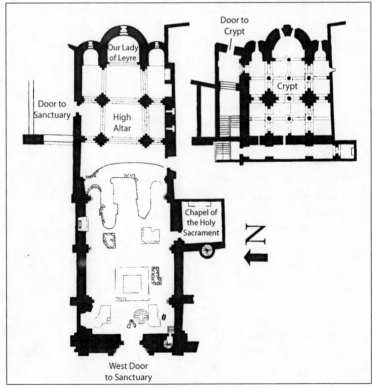

Plan of the church and crypt

the nearby reservoir, made by damming the Aragón River. Along with the natural beauty of the surroundings, the monastery buildings themselves offer much that is of interest.

The Crypt

The area beneath the east part of the church contains a crypt of unusual style (although it now functions as a crypt, it was originally an above-ground chapel.) This eleventh-century crypt is a forest of pillars and arches, some of which were installed to support the great weight of the church that was subsequently built over it. Short, thick columns arise from the floor and are capped by oversized capitals at waist height. Some of these capitals are plain but others are carved with intriguing patterns. The crypt is nearly square, with three apses at the end that correspond to the apses in the church above.

A group of us activated this space by walking in a clockwise (sunwise) direction. While some continued walking, others stood in the four corners and one person touched the central column. If you are with a group of like-minded persons, you can try to do the same. We experienced enhanced energy, which manifested itself by a subtle increase in light in the space and an enhanced feeling of well being. We sense that activating sacred spaces benefits more than our-

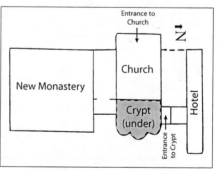

Plan for touring the monastery

selves. Spaces thus activated retain their enhanced energy for some time afterward, which may be sensed by those who come later.

The Church

The eleventh-twelfth century church is notable for its height; its stone walls are built of huge white limestone ashlars. It blends round Ro-

Interior of the church

manesque arches in the nave and pointed Gothic arches in the ceiling above. Far from being an incongruous mixture, the whole ensemble melds beautifully. There is a single Gothic flying buttress outside the north wall, although the rest of the outside looks more Romanesque in construction.

Of particular interest is the west door of the sanctuary, which has an impressive tympanum filled with elaborate carvings, and the Chapel of the Holy Sacrament with the seventeenth-century altarpiece of Saints Nunilo and Alodia. While in the chapel don't forget to look at the bosses in the ceiling. Can you sense the energy in the spiraling designs?

St. Virila's Fountain

On a hillside above the monastery is a fountain dedicated to St. Virila, reached by walking the marked trail

The nightingale at the fountain

from the parking lot. The trail passes through beautiful woods, and the view of the monastery and surrounding countryside is delightful. Spend some time in meditation at the fountain. Pay particular attention to the bird carved on a plaque near the fountain.

A legend states that St. Virila, abbot of the Monastery of Leyre in the late tenth century, worried how one could be happy throughout eternity in heaven. [In one version of the legend he was contemplating Psalm 89 (90 in Protestant Bibles) "Quoniam mille ante oculos tuos . . ." (For a thousand years in your sight are like a day that has just gone by . . .)] While walking on the grounds of the monastery he heard the song of a nightingale and was entranced, following it up to the fountain in the hills above, where he sat down in meditation. After some time he regained his senses and returned to the monastery—only to find that he knew no one there, nor did they know him. Finally an old monk remembered a letter he had found in an ancient book (in one version it is a Koran) about the disappearance long before of Abbot Virila.

There was considerable consternation in the monastery since there was already an abbot, and indeed, there had

The view from the hill back to the monastery

been several abbots since the time of Abbot Virila over one hundred (or perhaps three hundred) years before.

At this point the voice of God was heard: "If a hundred years passed while you were listening to the song of a nightingale, imagine how you will spend eternity with the Almighty." Thus Abbot Virila's doubts about being happy in heaven were removed. In one version of the story the nightingale then flew down from a tree carrying the abbot's ring and presented it to St. Virila, thus confirming that he was the true abbot of the monastery.

Once, when Elyn was visiting the fountain with a group, a small bird flew down and perched near the fountain for some time, entrancing everyone. However, when they returned to the monastery below it was still the same day—much to their relief.

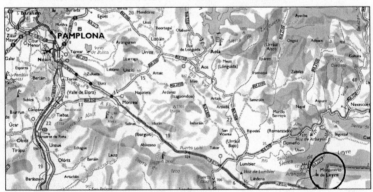

Map of the area

Getting There

Drive southeast out of Pamplona on N-240 (you can take A-21 part of the way) for approximately 31 miles. Turn on NA-2113 to Leyre. You must purchase a ticket to enter the crypt and visit the church. To do so, go to the gift shop at the entrance to the crypt.

Notes

Elyn Aviva

View down to Yuso from the monastery of Suso

San Millán de la Cogolla (Suso), La Rioja

I know that hermits have always sought isolated places for their lives of prayer, but San Millán of the Hood (or maybe of the Hillside) went further than most. He lived in a cave, perched high on a wooded hillside, far from the hustle and bustle of medieval civilization. A sanctified life, a sanctified death. A Visigothic church was built over his cave-like retreat. The entrance is lined with the sarcophagi of those who longed to be buried near the saint, as if his holiness was something they could share vicariously. Perhaps it was. Perhaps it is. (Elyn)

The twin monasteries of Yuso and Suso in the small town of San Millán de la Cogolla have an interesting history. Suso, which refers to "upper," is high up on a hillside and is the older of the two. It has been in existence since the sixth century CE. Yuso, which refers to "lower," is down in the valley below. It was founded 500 years later than Suso, although the present buildings are of sixteenth and seventeenth century origin.

A legend states that in the eleventh century the relics of San Millán, the saint of Suso, were being transported to a distant monastery when the oxen pulling the cart stopped in the valley and refused to continue. King García Sánchez took this as a sign from the saint and ordered a new monastery be constructed on the spot. The two monasteries coexisted for many centuries, but Suso was subject to the ecclesiastical confiscations of Mendizábal (the disentailment) in the early nineteenth century and has not been occupied since.

San Millán (also known as Saint Aemilian, Emilianus, Aemilianus, or San Millán de la Cogolla) was born in Berceo in La Rioja, Spain, around 472 CE. He is described as a shepherd who became a hermit at the age of twenty as the result of a sudden religious conversion. Didymus, the Bishop of Tarazona, called him to be a priest, but the clerical life did not suit him. He returned to the mountains and established the hermitage that later became the Monastery of

San Millán

Suso. He attracted a large following among the laity, and a monastic community developed around him. San Millán died around 573 CE and was buried in his cell at the hermitage.

The monastery of Suso was renowned as a seat of learning. The scriptorium, which remained active for most of its history, produced many important manuscripts. One such manuscript contains the first written examples of the Spanish and Basque languages. In 1997 UNESCO declared both monasteries a World Heritage Site in recognition of their im-

*Manuscript page
with note in Spanish
in the lower right corner*

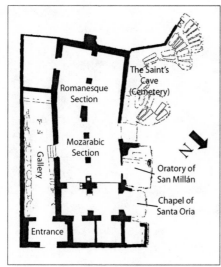

Suso floor plan

portance as the cradle of the Spanish language.

Over the centuries Suso became a *de facto* cemetery due to the large number of people who wished to be buried near San Millán. The gallery just inside the entrance hall is lined on both sides with the sarcophagi of the Seven Infantes of Lara and of three queens of Navarre: Elvira, Ximena, and Tota. San Millán's cave in the west corner of the monastery is also filled with sarcophagi. San Millán's remains were placed in the oratory until their removal to Yuso in the eleventh century.

The energetic center of Suso is the Saint's Oratory, where San Millán prayed in silence for forty years and where he was entombed. You can still feel the presence of the saint after more than nine centuries. If you can (there is an ever-present guide), try to meditate at the entrance of the oratory. Choose a time when the tour group is in another part of the building so you can be

Alabaster capitals in Suso

alone with San Millán. We experienced an intense wave of spiritual energy there that remained with us when we returned to the valley below. We found that the feeling could be maintained by following the saint's example and remaining in silence for a period of time.

Being present to a sacred place, like being present to everything else in life, requires attention. The first requisite is outer silence—you cannot be truly present while talking. Saints and other seekers often maintain silence as a discipline for long periods of time. A second, and more challenging, requisite is inner silence. Stilling the constant stream of thoughts requires discipline. Most spiritual traditions recommend specific practices to accomplish this.

Other Things to Do

The Monastery of Yuso has a museum with more than 300 handwritten manuscripts and various Romanesque ivories. You can also visit the church and the cloister, which are a mixture of Romanesque and Gothic styles. One section of the monastery has been turned into a hotel and restaurant. Several other inns and restaurants are also available.

Getting There

In order to visit Suso, you *must* purchase a ticket at Yuso (wise to reserve online in advance!) and ride (or walk) up in the shuttle bus, which leaves every half hour or so from near the ticket office. (Google: San Millan de la Cogolla)

Drive to Yuso from Santo Domingo de la Calzada on LR-204 through Cirueña to Villar de Torre. In Villar de Torre turn right on LR-206 to Berceo (San Millán's birthplace). From Berceo take LR-331

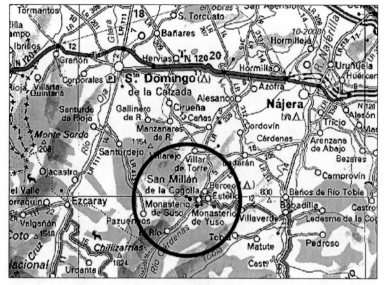

Area map

to San Millán de la Cogolla. There is ample parking across the street from Yuso.

A hiking trail leads up the hill from Yuso to Suso, but it is steep. You might consider walking one way and taking the shuttle bus in the other direction. The trail goes through some beautiful woods and is well worth your time. There are also other trails in the vicinity.

Notes

Elyn Aviva

Interior of San Baudelio, view from the apse

Ermita de San Baudelio de Berlanga, Soria Province, Castilla y León

The Hermitage of San Baudelio stands on an isolated hilltop. It is an intriguing, box-shaped building, its plain walls broken only by an unadorned horseshoe-arched doorway. A smaller box-shaped room is attached at one end. How simple and austere it looks, surrounded by grey limestone-conglomerate boulders and patches of grass. The simplicity, however, is a clever disguise. Cross the threshold and you enter a fantastic realm. In the center of the building is the massive soaring trunk of a stone palm tree, a veritable Tree of Life, its eight branches spreading across the ceiling high above. To your right, a low forest of arches supports a painted gallery above, and in the south corner, a rough-hewed entrance beckons you into a pitch-black grotto. Faint traces of painted cattle, a camel, elephants, ibis, a bear, hares, and hunting dogs cavort across the walls of the hermitage. High on an arch above the gallery, a clown-like figure leers down at you as he squats and exposes his private parts. To your left, stairs lead to the small apse, where an upside down dove painted above the narrow window dive-bombs the altar. (Elyn)

The shrine of San Baudelio is a tenth- or eleventh-century hermitage *(ermita)* with a unique mix of Christian and Mozarabic elements. It sits on a steep slope in an isolated area southwest of Soria, near the town of Berlanga de Duero. The building was constructed at the mouth of a cave, which was possibly used by a hermit. This grotto has several interconnecting chambers. The main part of the building is approximately 28' x 24', giving the building a nearly cubic appearance. Attached to the main building is the nearly square apse, which is reached by two steps leading through a horseshoe arch. The hermitage is oriented approximately 45° off the north-south axis, so the apse is in the northeast and the grotto is in the south. One writer has stated that the dimensions are organized by proportions related to the golden ratio (phi), but that has not been confirmed and the dimensions above do not appear to bear this out.

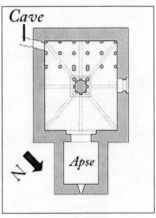

Floor plan of San Baudelio

The most puzzling aspect of the building is that the northeast half is clearly a Christian design, with a single nave ending in an apse. The southwest half, on the other hand, resembles a miniature mosque, complete with three rows of arches, each with six columns, and what could be a small *mihrab* (the niche in a mosque that indicates the direction toward Mecca) in the gallery above. This mix of Christian and Islamic elements is *most* unusual.

We are even led to speculate if this mixture is an indication of shared religious practice, since the hermitage lies very near the shifting border between Muslim and Christian lands in the tenth and eleventh centuries. This might also account for the nearly perfect preservation of the site in spite of successive waves

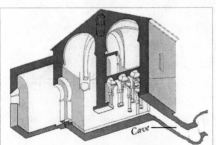

Elevation showing the cave

The ceiling of San Baudelio

of warfare. All this is speculation, since no one knows much about the early history of this sanctuary.

In the mid-twelfth century, gorgeous murals were painted over most of the interior surfaces. Unfortunately, many of these murals were sold to various museums in the early twentieth century (a long, sad story of greed and legal battles). To view these murals you would need to visit the Metropolitan Museum of Art in New York City, the Museum of Fine Arts in Boston, the Indianapolis Museum, and the Prado in Madrid, among others. Evocative traces of many of the paintings are still visible on the walls of the hermitage. Their faded remains mar the building from an aesthetic perspective but do little to affect the energies we sensed there.

Like other aspects of this building, the murals are a mix of Christian and Islamic themes. This has led scholars to postulate that the building might have been occupied by

Painting of a bull on the southeast wall

54

Christians and Muslims at different times. Christian themes showing scenes from the life of Christ (curing the blind, the three Marys before the tomb, etc.) contrast with exotic animals and hunting scenes. A large painting of a bear, which might be a reference to the Great Bear constellation (Big Dipper), stands to the right of the main entrance facing north. An ibis struts along one of the arches above the gallery, and

The arches in the southwest gallery

an elephant, a camel, bulls, and other animals adorn other walls.

The spring

Outside, a spring provides a supply of fresh water adequate to meet the needs of the monks who built the structure. We believe that the presence of subterranean water has something to do with the strong energy we sensed in the main building. Another factor, we believe, is the floor of the building, which is the limestone-conglomerate bedrock. When you stand in the nave, your feet are in contact with limestone that has subterranean water coursing under it. A number of researchers have found significant electrical energy is generated by water running through limestone.

Visiting the Hermitage

It is best to visit San Baudelio when there are no tour busses present. Our experience has been that tour busses are gone by late afternoon since they need to travel to their evening lodging. A guide is stationed at the site when it is open. He is most helpful and, after collecting a small admission fee, will give you the space you need to fully experience the site. He is knowledgeable but only speaks Spanish. (If you can engage him in a conversation, he has much to share about the building and its energies!)

In general, we find it helpful to make physical contact with a building before entering. Place your right hand on the door frame or a column at the entrance for a few seconds to harmonize yourself with the energy of the place. When you enter, take a few moments to stand in one place and sense what you are feeling. Then begin to move about the structure.

Pause before entering the hermitage in order to center yourself. We found the energy quite variable depending on where we were standing. Some areas seemed quite neutral while others were very strong. The energy under

Entrance to the cave in the south corner

Elyn Aviva

the forest of columns is particularly strong, as is the entry to the cave. Access to the gallery is not generally available to the public, since the interior stairs have no guardrail.

You can visit the cave at the rear of the building and the guide will provide a flashlight (offer him a tip). The cave is quite small and the floor is dirt over limestone. Be prepared to get dirty if you decide to go there. On one visit we found the energy inside the grotto to be calm and peaceful although the energy at the threshold was quite powerful. Another time, Elyn had the distinct sense she shouldn't disturb whatever energetic presence was there. She left immediately.

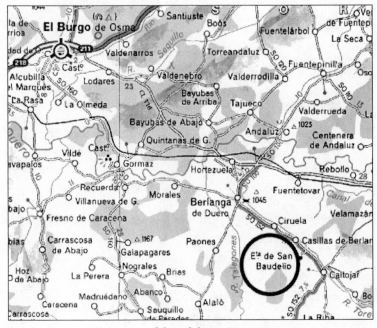

Map of the area

Getting There

Drive southeast from El Burgo de Osma on CL-116 (toward Almazán). Near Hortezuela turn right on SO-152 (toward Berlanga de Duero). Purple "historical site" signs posted near Berlanga will lead you to San Baudelio. The site is a few hundred yards off the highway on the right, up a fairly sharp incline. There is ample parking near the site if it is not crowded. (http://www.muselius.com/spain/soria/ermita-de-san-baudelio-de-berlanga/) You will find the spring to the right of the building. We are told that the water is quite good. It is cold and clear. A visit to the spring would also be a good way to harmonize with the site. You must purchase a ticket from the guide inside the entrance to the hermitage. He also has guidebooks for sale.

If the frescoes in San Baudelio interest you, you might want to visit the Hermitage of St. Michael (Ermita de San Miguel de Gormaz) nearby, which has impressive frescoes. It is located on the road to a massive ruined Moorish fortress. Ask the guide at San Baudelio for information.

Notes

Elyn Aviva

View of the hermitage from the cave

Ermita de San Bartolo in Cañón del Río Lobos, Ucero, Soria Province, Castilla y León

We follow the shady, half-mile-long trail that leads to the Hermitage of San Bartolomé (San Bartolo), said to be a Templar church hidden away for unknown reasons centuries ago. Trees line the banks of the Río Lobos, the River of the Wolves. Purple and yellow flowers proliferate; water lilies float in the slow-moving stream. Stunning limestone cliffs soar skyward on either side, eroded over millennia by the unrelenting, ever-patient river. Screaming Griffon vultures and silent eagles wheel above us, swooping and soaring in and out of the narrow canyon.

The hermitage suddenly comes into sight, nestling in the horseshoe bend of the river. An intriguing window on the south wall stands out, composed of a five-pointed, upside-down star (one point down, two up, two on either side). Adjacent star-points are joined by twin arcs, creating repetitive heart shapes. The star and hearts are enclosed within a circle. Five hearts, five star points woven out of stone. What meanings do they hide and what reveal? Across the river, an immense cave beckons. (Elyn)

The Hermitage of San Bartolo (or San Bartolomé) is in an isolated area of the Parque Natural del Cañón del Río Lobos. No road goes to it and probably never has, although it is reported that some pilgrims to Santiago passed through nearby Ucero (with its pilgrimage refuge) and the Canyon of Río Lobos en route to Burgo de Osma, where various routes came together and continued on to the Camino Francés, the main route across Spain. What is a church doing in this

60

isolated location? People have speculated and have proposed many theories. One is that the hermitage was built by the Knights Templar as a hiding place for some of their most important documents and arti-facts—a sort of medieval safety deposit box. That would seem to explain it, but why build a church? Because building a church was a subterfuge? Oth-ers say it was the site of secret Templar initiations. At any rate, it is a powerful place in a powerful setting.

As we walked toward the hermitage we were struck im-mediately by the round lattice window on the southeast wall. There are no impressive win-dows on the east or the west, where you usually see them in a church. Instead, there are two identical lattice windows, one on the north and one on the south. The heart/pen-tangle window is the first thing you see as you approach, as if to announce that this is not an ordinary church.

"In the heart of the province of Soria, far from all com-mercial routes and the Pil-grims' Way, in a wild canyon along the Lobos River, there rises a small, transitional Ro-manesque church built next to the enormous mouth of a cave where, not so long ago, important prehistoric re-mains were discovered. This little church is all that is left of one of the most impor-tant Templar *encomiendas* of Castile, cited in texts such as that of San Juan de Otero. As recorded in a handful of documents, this and other locations were acquired by the Order during the last quarter of the twelfth centu-ry." Juan García Atienza. *The Knights Templar in the Golden Age of Spain*. Rochester, Ver-mont: Destiny Books, 2001, p. 261.

The window contains ten hearts—five large ones, inter-twined, and five small ones

Elyn Aviva

The "heart" window

Perhaps the intriguing window design represents the Divine Spark in the heart of each of us—and the balance and perfection for which we can seek. What the builders had in mind we'll never know, but what they have left behind in the lattice windows of San Bartolomé is worthy of extensive contemplation.

around the rim. Or perhaps those were an afterthought, formed out of a pentangle with a pentagon in its center. It all depends on how you look at it. Although today the upside-down pentangle is sometimes associated with Satanism, that is a fairly recent connection, proposed in the late nineteenth century by Eliphas Levi. It's safe to say that when the window was constructed (probably by Muslim Mudéjar workmen in the thirteenth century), the pentangle had no such meaning. In fact, for the Sumerians it had astrological associations; for the Pythagoreans it represented the Greek goddess of health, and they attributed mathematical perfection to it.

Given the Islamic connection, it's worth looking at the meaning of the heart in Sufism, the mystical tradition of Islam. Sufis believe that the heart is the medium through which one achieves true knowledge, the intuitive comprehension or understanding of God. To the Sufi, the heart of the believer is like a mirror that reflects the Eternal Light and sublime consciousness.

Here, at San Bartolomé, we have not one but five—or even ten—hearts, as well as the five-pointed star and pentagon. Which point us to another question, that of the significance of the numbers five and ten.

Elyn Aviva

The view of the hermitage as you approach

The hermitage is built directly on projecting bedrock, a limestone-conglomerate mass at the center of the horseshoe bend of the Río Lobos. The solid stone seems to radiate energy, per-

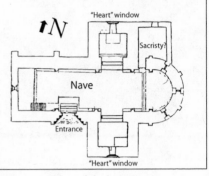

Plan of the hermitage

haps because of the swirling river on three sides of it. We have experienced considerable energy in sites like this when a building is placed directly on the bedrock, particularly if there is a source of moving water nearby (see San Baudelio, p. 50). The surrounding cliff seems to reflect the energy back to the building, which lies at the focal point. And then there is the huge cave just across the river, whose gaping entrance faces directly toward the church. All factors conspire to concentrate energy directly on the building.

The building was closed when we were there, so our observations are limited to the external aspects of the site. We experienced considerable energy as we climbed up the projecting stone embankment to the entrance of the building. We walked around the building as best we could, given the terrain; the energy seemed to increase as we ap-

Some investigators have proposed an intriguing relationship between San Bartolo and other locations. It is equidistant from the two extreme northern points of the peninsula: Finisterre on the west and Cap de Creus on the east. Others claim it is the center of a Maltese cross (purported to be the Templar cross) whose tips touch various Templar possessions—making San Bartolo a kind of occult *axis mundi* or *omphalos* (world center) for the Templars in Spain.

Five often represents the human as microcosmos (legs and arms outstretched, inscribed in a pentagon). We have five fingers on each hand, five toes on each foot, and so on. Five also represents the "golden number," a particularly pleasing proportion; and in alchemy, it represents (among other things) the quintessence or ether—from which the other four elements arise. It is also said to represent the perfect union of feminine (2) and masculine (3). Five small hearts and five large ones add up to ten, considered a "divine" number that represents totality, completion, and return to unity. It also represents perfection.

proached the small room that had been added on the back side (labeled "Sacristy?" in the drawing). We noted that this small room was facing directly toward the cave and wondered if that might account for the energy we were experiencing. Walk around the site and see what you experience.

The cave across the river is over fifty feet in height but not very deep. There are prehistoric pictographs inside, which indicate ancient human settlement in the area and suggest the cave was an ancient sacred site. This area is a favorite picnic locale and groups of visitors could be heard singing and shouting in the cave nearly all the time we were there. We

Cave at Río Lobos

waited until the cave was deserted before entering. Our perceptions were colored by the recent activity in the cave, but we felt a sense of irritation, as if the once-honored cave resented the loud, abusive visitors. Perhaps you will have a different experience.

The Poor Fellow-Soldiers of Christ and of the Temple of Solomon (Knights Templar), a Western Christian military order, was founded in the late eleventh century, purportedly to protect Christian pilgrims who were en route to the Holy Land. During the following two centuries the Order gained much wealth and property in France and Spain. It is often said that they were the first international bankers due to their ability to transfer cash all over the European continent. Their wealth and power attracted many enemies, including the king of France. On Friday, October 13, 1307, King Philip of France had the Templars arrested, tortured, and tried for various offenses, thus putting an end to the order (and perhaps starting the negative associations with Friday the thirteenth). In recent centuries they have become the stuff of novels and alternative history books.

Other Things to Do

The Parque Natural del Cañón del Río Lobos is well known as a marvelous nature preserve. The cliffs are nesting places for many bird species including eagle owls, Egyptian and Griffon vultures, and golden eagles. An extensive system of trails through pine and juniper forests is available for those who want an outdoor experience. Caves dot the high cliffs and some are accessible for visits. (Google: parque natural del cañon rio lobos for information or go to: http://www.rutasyviajes.net/cl/burgos/riolobos/riolobos.html for detailed maps.)

There is also a Templar castle in the nearby town of Ucero that is worth a visit. (Google: templar castle ucero)

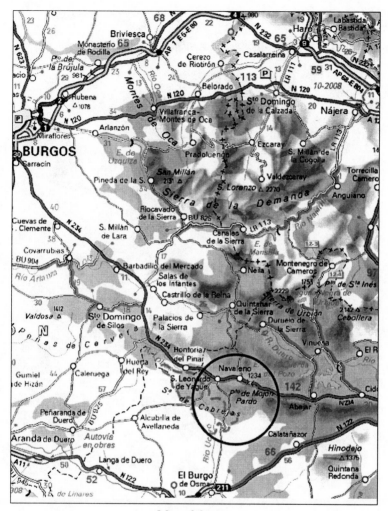

Map of the area

Getting There

   The Parque Natural del Cañón del Río Lobos is located between Burgos and Soria, just off of N-234. Drive 47 miles from Burgos to San Leonardo de Yagüe and turn on SO-934 to SO-920 toward Burgo de Osma. Just outside of Ucero turn into the Parque

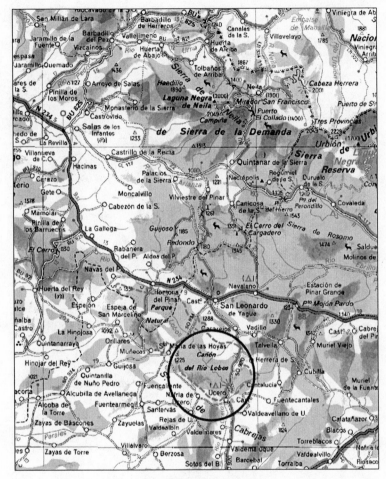

Detailed map of the park

Natural del Cañón del Río Lobos. The road ends at a campground, where you can park. You will see signs showing two ways to walk to the hermitage. The one on the left is longer, but flat; the one on the right is shorter, but climbs a bit. We have walked both trails and find the one on the left gives you a better view of the hermitage than the one on the right. Neither walk is very long.

The Hermitage of San Bartolo is not regularly open (Google: parque natural del cañon rio lobos to find information about open hours). However, a walk in the park is worthwhile even if you can't get inside the building.

Notes

Elyn Aviva

The Dolmen de Cubillejo

Dolmen de Cubillejo and Santa María de Lara, Quintanilla de las Viñas, Burgos Province, Castilla y León

In the middle of a field, far from settlement, the Dolmen de Cubillejo remains more or less intact. Its earthen cover-

ing is long gone, as are all but one capstone. But the upright sides remain, part-hidden in the earth, and the long passageway, and one capstone. We bow under it to enter the central chamber, an unavoidable posture that somehow becomes a ritual act. Birth canal and womb, church nave and sanctuary. The form repeats itself. Entrance into life—and death. Two well-worn petro-

View from inside the central chamber

glyphs adorn the passage, their meaning obscure—or perhaps obscured. Who knows who watches still.

We drive on. The setting is spectacular. Isolation, distant hills with beckoning caves. A ruined castle, Roman remains, a Visigothic hermitage. Millennia of history unfold around. Birds wheel and screech in the sky. A distant storm threatens.

We head up the nearaby ridge on foot. Eventually the view expands 360°. Space above, space below, space all around. Breathe deep. Breathe deep again, reaching out to the hills around. I didn't make it to the caves (the way became too exposed, too rocky), but several of our group climbed on—and up to the top of the bluff, aided by guide ropes along the path. Their reward was great: traces of ancient settlement, a quartz pillar standing up against the sky. I waited below. The rain began to splatter all around. I headed down the slippery, red-blazoned trail.... (Elyn)

The area around the hamlets of Cubillejo and Quintanilla de las Viñas is filled with signs of millennia of human habitation. The oldest, by far, is the Dolmen de Cubillejo, which may be as much as five thousand years old. This passage "tomb" has a long, thirty-foot entry passage leading to a nearly circular inner chamber. One of the stones along the corridor is decorated with petroglyphs, as are the stones in many dolmens throughout Europe. The

"The English author and dowser Paul Devereux calls these sites 'places of geographical sanctity,' the later Romans named the mysterious power found at such places the *genius loci*, or the spirit of the place. A spirit that is still tangible at many Neolithic sites today. Indeed many sensitive people report a subtle but distinct shift in consciousness that occurs when visiting sites such as Stonehenge, Avebury, Silbury Hill, or Newgrange. Therefore the question that naturally arises is this: Does such a shift in consciousness arise as a result of the *genius loci*, the telluric power of such places, or as a result of the symbolic effect of the structure itself? Or, indeed, is it some strange combination of at least those two factors among possible and, as yet, undefined, others?" Tim Wallace-Murphy. *Cracking the Symbol Code: Revealing the Secret Heretical Messages within Church and Renaissance Art.* London: Watkins Publishing, 2005, p. 8.

passageway faces south-east, as do many dolmens, opening in the direction of the rising sun at winter solstice. No one knows exactly why this orientation was important to the megalith builders, but it clearly was. One can imagine. . . .

For that matter, no one knows exactly what these structures were used for, but since they often have human bones in them, people have called them tombs. That is like calling Westminster Abbey a tomb because important people are buried there.

Originally, the Dolmen of Cubillejo had capstones over the corridor and over the circular chamber at the end. The entire structure was covered with earth (and perhaps stones) to make a mound. One had to crawl on hands and knees to enter. The covering has disappeared in the five thousand years of the dolmen's

Satellite photo of the area

72

existence, leaving only the bare skeleton of the central structure.

The builders spent an enormous amount of time and effort constructing these dolmens, using only their muscles and a few simple tools for the task. The dolmens must have been very important. We believe they were ritual centers for the megalith builders and should be respected as such. In addition, geomancers say that dolmens could be used energetically to improve crop production or perhaps to enhance general well-being.

The Dolmen de Cubillejo still radiates considerable energy if approached in the right way. Treat it as you would any sacred space. Take time to orient yourself by placing your right hand on the stone at the entry. Then enter the passageway, taking time to sense what you are feeling. Does it change once you bow beneath the capstone and enter the central chamber? Take time to meditate there.

Santa María de Lara

The eighth-century Visigothic church of Santa María de Lara near the neighboring town of Quintanilla de las Viñas is remarkable for several reasons. The

first thing you notice is that there is no mortar between the stones of this building. This dry-stone construction relies on exact fitting of the surfaces of the

Santa María de Lara

stones. You will also notice the bands of contrasting colored stone that run around the building. The lighter bands are extensively carved with floral and animal designs, most of which are contained in circles.

Santa María de Lara has gone through many alterations. What remains is the apse with its beautifully decorated horseshoe arch and a central part of the crossing of the later Latin-cross addition. The nave and the extensions of the transept are gone and are represented only by the outlines of foundations on the ground. Long in ruins, what was left of the church was restored in the twentieth century and given a protective wooden roof.

"One of the most important of the Germanic peoples, the Visigoths separated from the Ostrogoths in the 4th century CE, raided Roman territories repeatedly, and established great kingdoms in Gaul and Spain. The Visigoths were settled agriculturists in Dacia (now in Romania) when they were attacked by the Huns in 376 and driven southward across the Danube River into the Roman Empire. They were allowed to enter the empire, but the exactions of Roman officials soon drove them to revolt and plunder the Balkan provinces, assisted by some Ostrogoths. On Aug. 9, 378, they utterly defeated the army of the Roman emperor Valens on the plains outside Adrianople, killing the emperor himself. For four more years they continued to wander in search of somewhere to settle. In October 382 Valens' successor, Theodosius I, settled them in Moesia (in the Balkans) as federates, giving them land there and imposing on them the duty of defending the frontier. It was apparently during this period that the Visigoths were converted to Arian Christianity. They remained in Moesia until 395, when, under the leadership of Alaric, they left Moesia and moved first southward into Greece and then to Italy, which they invaded repeatedly from 401 onward. Their depredations culminated in the sack of Rome in 410. In the same year Alaric died and was succeeded by Ataulphus, who led the Visigoths to settle first in southern Gaul, then in Spain (415)." *Britannica Online Encyclopedia.*

74

The carvings are noteworthy for their quality and the subject matter represented. Inside the church, on the left of the apse, is a carving of a bearded man's face topped by a lunar symbol; on the right is a female

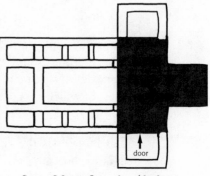

Santa María floor plan (dark area is the current building)

face wearing a crown of sun-rays. This is a reversal of the usual symbology, in which females are equat-

The moon symbol

ed with the moon and males with the sun—but this was not an uncommon pattern among Germanic tribes. Both of these heads are inside rings held by angels. A large sculpted stone in the apse has a central figure that may represent Christ, flanked by angels. All the carvings, both on the exterior and interior of the building, are remarkable for their detail and unified style. We've been told you can "hear" some of the interior

The sun symbol

The carved stone "table"

columns vibrate at a certain pitch.

Santa María de Lara is kept locked due to the theft of some of the stone carvings. Inquire in the village for a guide if you want to see the interior.

The Caves and the Hill

In the bluff facing the church are a series of caves, probably once inhabited by hermits. The caves are reachable if you are not afraid of heights. The trail to the caves begins at Santa María and snakes up the hillside in a series of switchbacks. While most of the trail is rather steep, it is only the final section that is really exposed. The view is quite impressive—including the ruined medieval castle of Lara de los Infantes. At one point the waymarked trail splits and you can walk to the castle instead of the caves.

Just before reaching the caves, you can take a precipitous trail that leads up (with the help of guide ropes) to the top of the bluff. Here are the remains of a small settlement and an unusual white quartz pillar. The view of the valley below is spectacular.

The caves

Other Things to Do

There are many way-marked hiking trails in the region of Cubillejo and Quintanilla. The GR-82 passes by the church of Santa María de Lara. You can find information at http://www.sierradelademanda.com/es/archivodigital/index.asp, which leads to Google Earth maps of the area. The section ETAPA6-Palazuelos de la Sierra-Covarrubias passes through this area.

Getting There

The Dolmen de Cubillejo and Santa María de Lara are just off the N-234 between Burgos and Soria. The hamlets of Cubillejo and Quintanilla de las Viñas

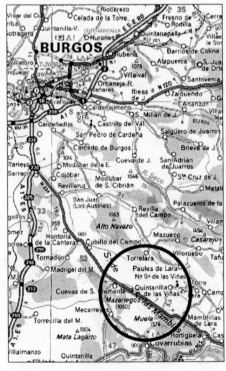

are shown on most maps, but the road you will need to drive may not be. Take the N-234 from Burgos to Soria. Go through Quintanilla de las Viñas to the village of Cubillejo de Lara. On the outskirts of the village (direction Cuevas de San Clemente) there is a dirt road on the left-hand side that is marked on the satellite photo on page 71. It has a small sign

Map of the area

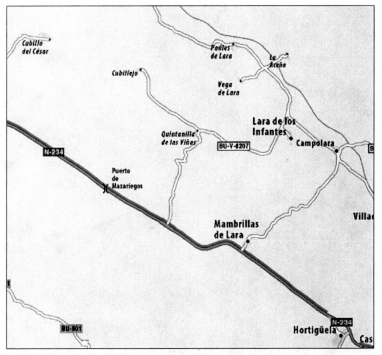

Detailed map of the area

pointing to the dolmen. Take that road (perfectly fine for cars) and continue to the second crossroads (a power line is very close). There, on the right hand side is the dolmen. You'll see an information sign near the road.

To drive to Santa María de Lara, follow the road signs to Quintanilla de las Viñas. Santa María is just outside of town.

Notes

Santa Cristina de Lena

Santa Cristina de Lena, Pola de Lena, Asturias

Imagine yourself a medieval pilgrim, wandering for days on the Camino de San Salvador that leads you through the high mountain passes of the Cantrabricans, losing your way, finding it again. You are weary, alone. Only faith and hope keep you going. Suddenly you see before you what looks like a mirage: the church of Santa Cristina de Lena beckoning from a distant hilltop. Your strength renewed you draw near, following the old Roman road that continues on to Oviedo and the chapel that contains the holy face-cloth of Jesus. You draw close to the ninth-century church, its stones glowing in the setting sun, and you give heartfelt thanks before the altar. (Elyn)

Santa Cristina de Lena stands on the brow of a steep hill twenty-five miles south of Oviedo, in the province of Asturias. It is a jewel of Asturian-Visigothic architecture, a distinction that was recognized in 1985 when it was added to UNESCO's World Heritage list of protected monuments. Dating from the early ninth century when the Visigothic king Ramiro I reigned in Oviedo, the building shows some similarity to other Visigothic buildings in Germany and elsewhere in Europe.

The approach to Santa Cristina de Lena is along a tree-lined path with sheep grazing on the grass. This setting creates a picture of an idealized, bucolic church. It's a suitably evocative location for an evocative church, full of unusual interior features and a great sense of mystery and power.

The church has five rectangular spaces: a small, nearly square room is attached to each of the four sides of the larger, higher rectangular central room. Together, they form a sort of equal-armed cross.

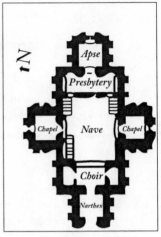

The central room includes the nave, a raised platform in the east, and an overhead choir in the west. The square addition on the east side forms the apse, while the one on the west side (behind and below the choir) is the vestibule or narthex. Those on the north and south are small chapels. The church has only a few

Floor plan of Santa Cristina de Lena

When Elyn and I first started visiting powerful places together, she would sometimes say that she "saw something." She described it as being like a subtle smoke or fog. I would not see what she was seeing, but I trusted that she was able to see things that I couldn't. Then there came a day when I began to see this "ectoplasm" myself. What had changed? Of course, it was me. I had changed. I think that the years of doing regular (and sometimes not-so-regular) meditation practices contributed to my expanded vision. The primary change, however, was that I began to look in a different way.

Monet said that he tried to paint the light in a scene, not the objects. By painting the same scene in different conditions of light, he was able to depict light itself. The objects in the scene became a mere background. I would say that I have begun to look at the space in a sacred place, as well as at the solid objects. I would describe this as shifting my focus. Some might say that I have unfocused my eyes, but that would assume that I am still looking at the objects in front of me—and that is not the case. Try "looking at the air" and see what you see. It will take some practice. Santa Cristina de Lena is a good place to start. (Gary)

small windows: one in each of the side additions, two on the north and south walls, and two high windows on the east and west of the main building. The windows provide adequate but minimal light. The general atmosphere is subdued.

The arcade and altar in the apse viewed from the choir

You enter the church from the west, passing from the narthex into the nave. Take some time to feel the atmosphere of the place and to let your eyes adjust to the low light. Several unusual features will quickly become apparent. At the east end of the nave is a raised platform, reached by seven (note: seven!) steps on the left and right of the room. This presbytery is set off from the main room by an ornate triple arcade supported by four marble columns. The top of the arcade is decorated with lattice work and carved rectangles. The space between the two center columns is blocked with three slabs of marble about three feet in height; they are recycled funerary stones and bear the inscription, "in this site was buried Telius in . . . March, in the era of 681 (643 CE)." It is thought that this arcade was a later addition to the church and used to screen some parts of

The marble slabs in the screen

the priest's preparation of the bread and wine from the congregation. This raised platform and arcade appear to be unique in pre-Romanesque (Visigothic) architecture.

One of the medallions

Beyond the platform three (note: three!) steps lead to the apse.

In the west of the central room is the overhead choir, reached by a single set of stairs along the north wall. There is evidence that a second set of stairs on the south wall was removed at some time in the past. This staircase would have given the room balanced symmetry.

Elyn in one of the small side rooms

The walls of the church have circular medallions; carved animals and geometrical motifs adorn the capitals of some of the columns.

On the main floor under the choir are two very small rooms, one on either side. They are entered through low arched doors. The purpose of these

Elyn Aviva

The cave

rooms is unknown. They can only be entered by crawling on your hands and knees. Elyn entered one of these spaces and reported that the ceiling was much taller than the low door would suggest. Storage rooms? Meditation spaces? Who knows . . . .

We dowsed the church for energy lines and found several interesting crossings. There is evidence that underground water is responsible for some of the power we felt in this church. When we mentioned this possibility to Inez, the custodian, she told us that there was a cave outside and under the church (the entrance of which is now gated and locked). In the past, when she had gone into the cave she always heard running water. We were not able to confirm this, of course, but it is consistent with what we found using dowsing rods, and a stream flows through the valley below.

Visigothic architecture (also called pre-Romanesque in Spain) is characterized by extensive use of ashlar (large block) construction, sometimes without mortar, absence or sobriety of exterior decoration, floor plans segmented into small, discontinuous spaces, Islamic-style horseshoe arches, stylized vegetable decoration, and the use of columns crowned by Corinthian capitals for support. Examples include San Miguel de Escalada in León, San Baudelio de Berlanga in Soria (see p. 50), San Millán de Suso in La Rioja (see p. 44), Santa Cristina de Lena in Asturias, and San Julián de Los Prados and the Palace of Santa María de Naranco in Oviedo.

Santa Cristina de Lena has undergone considerable alteration over the centuries. Frescoes on the walls were unfortunately removed in a misguided nineteenth-century restoration. The architect Lázaro reported in 1894 that he had "completely scrape(d) off the whitewash of the building," presumably unintentionally

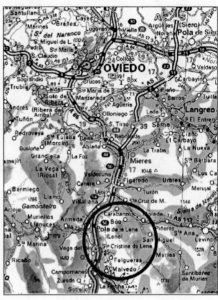

Area map

destroying the priceless frescoes. It is thought that the small chapels on each side might have been later additions. They may have been added to create a cross

design for a church that originally was a rectangle. In the nineteenth century a belfry was added to the building (and to many other churches in Spain), but that addition has now been removed. What you see now is the best approximation of what the church may have looked like for most

Detailed map

of its existence—except, of course, for the priceless missing frescoes.

The custodian, Inez, is very pleasant and knowledgeable. Open hours are posted on a sign at the foot of the hill below the church, but be prepared for some flexibility in this schedule. Santa Cristina de Lena is in a very isolated place and the number of visitors is not large.

Getting There

Drive A-66 south from Oviedo (or north from León), taking exit 59 to AS-242. After Pola de Lena turn left on LN-4 and drive up the hill to the almost-non-existent hamlet of Palacio. There is parking near the path to Santa Cristina de Lena. This path is the original Roman road, now known as the Camino de San Salvador. The walk is not long and it is beautiful; it sets the mood for arriving like a pilgrim at the church. If you would like to visit the cave described above after visiting the church, continue on the steep path down the hill. The cave is on the left not far below. Alternatively, you can park your car in the parking lot at the base of the hill and follow the steep trail that leads directly up the hill to the church.

Other Things to Do

Oviedo has a number of interesting places to see, including the cathedral—especially its Cámara Santa and the eerie crypt of San Leocadia accessed through the cloister; the church of San Julián de Los Prados with wonderful pre-Romanesque frescoes; and the Palacio de Santa María de Naranco on a hill above the city.

Elyn Aviva

The sanctuary of San Andrés de Teixido

San Andrés de Teixido, A Coruña Province, Galicia

I strolled down the narrow lane lined with souvenir stands selling wax milagros, *then past the small, tidy sanctuary that guards the relics of Saint Andrew, the apostle, pausing briefly at the three-spouted holy well in the shaded grove below. The path led on. Where, I wondered? I walked faster now, drawn by mystery, pulled by the distant roar of the sea. What's this? White specks dotted a fence and trees. These are clootie cloths, popular in Celtic lands around sacred wells: prayers and promises, hopes and healing, impressed on a piece of white cloth or rag and tied around a ready receptacle.... Why here? Why now?*

I slid through the narrow, clootie-covered gate and hurried down the sloping path that led through a green meadow, then climbed down a short ladder to the meadow below. The sea still called; mystery still drew me on. I lowered myself carefully down a stone wall to yet another meadow and followed the ever-downward path until it ended abruptly at a row of white-dotted bushes. An evergreen forest beckoned on one side, boulders and a grove of gnarled trees beckoned on the other. Waves frothed and battered against the precipitous cliffs far below.... A fresh breeze ruffled the clootie cloths. I inhaled the scent of pine.

Suddenly everything except the sea became very, very still. I held my breath, afraid to turn around. (Elyn)

San Andrés de Teixido (tay-SHEE-doe) is a major pilgrimage shrine tucked away in the far northwest corner of Galicia. The raw natural beauty of this

88

place is spectacular. You really must go there to fully appreciate its elemental power. For centuries, pilgrims have been drawn to the shrine, lured by the saying, "Que quien no va de vivo, va de muerto"—"If you don't go there in this life, your soul will have to go there in the next." The idea of a soul traversing the earth after death in the form of a snake, a toad, or a lizard is far from orthodox Catholic belief but very much in the spirit of Celtic Galicia.

In language, history, and spirit, Galicia is unlike the rest of Spain. This is a land that looks toward the Celtic world—Ireland, Scotland, Brittany—rather than to Castilla or León. Magic is alive and well here, giving this powerful place great intensity.

There is evidence of Neolithic settlement over 4000 years ago. Celtic people arrived in Galicia 2500 years

"Another legend tells that San Andrés was still unhappy because very few visited his church whereas thousands went to that of his fellow apostle, Santiago. One time, Christ was traveling the land with St Peter. On arriving in Teixido, he was thirsty and opened an apple. He encountered San Andrés inside, who complained about the slight attendance at his hermitage and begged that he be taken from that deserted place and taken to somewhere less inhospitable. Then Christ, feeling sorry for him, made a fountain spring forth and promised that nobody would enter into heaven if they hadn't made the pilgrimage to Teixido. From this comes the saying, "a San Andrés de Teixido va de muerto quien no van de vivo" (One goes after death to San Andrés if one didn't go while alive")—or, according to one version, you will have to go at least three times after death! There are those who believe that going on pilgrimage seven times to Teixido guarantees eternal glory." Xosé Ramón Mariño Ferro. *Santuarios Mágicos de Galicia*. Pontevedra: Colección Andaina, 2003, p. 17 (translation by Elyn Aviva).

"Water is the primary symbol of life: it is the source of vitality, for without it life cannot exist. Because of this, water, and most especially water sources, have been revered since the earliest times. In Celtic belief, natural waters—springs, streams, rivers, ponds, and lakes—are ensouled with indwelling spirits which must be acknowledged and nurtured." Nigel Pennick. *Celtic Sacred Landscapes*. New York: Thames & Hudson, 1996, p. 63.

ago. Many local legends are of Celtic origin, including the idea that Christian saints "came by sea," which harkens back to the Celtic belief in an Other World over the waters. To Celtic people the Other World isn't just a place of death but also a place of life, inhabited by heros and gods as well as the dead. Legends assert that many souls travel through Galicia on their way to the "Más Allá" (the "Land Beyond"), the doorway to the Other World.

The Norse god Odin was the god of magic and knowledge who guided souls in their afterlife journey to the Other World. (Vikings invaded Galicia in the ninth century.) The yew tree (known in Galicia as the *tejo* or *teixo*) is consecrated to the god Odin—and the "Teixido" in San Andrés de Teixido refers to the yew tree. The yew was also one of the Druids' sacred trees.

The Church

There was a monastery in Teixido in the twelfth century, but the earliest written record of the sanctuary of San Andrés de Teixido is 1391. The present church was built in the sixteenth and eighteenth centuries. It is considered the second most important shrine in Galicia, second only to the cathedral in Santiago de Compostela. The Camino Inglés from Ferrol to Santiago has an extension that leads north to Teixido. (http://www.valdovino.com/comun/SUB-PAGINAS/sanandres.html)

For centuries pilgrims walked a tortuous path to reach the shrine, and they built numerous *milladoiros* (rock piles) by bringing a stone and leaving it behind. This custom is found in other Celtic lands as well. The Cruz de Ferro (the rock pile west of Astorga on the Camino de Santiago) was originally a mound of stones dedicated to Hermes, patron of travelers and crossroads.

Interior of the church; note wax ex votos

Elyn Aviva

San Andrés is known as a healing shrine, and thousands come on pilgrimage throughout the year. Ex votos (wax or bread figures of body parts) are sold in the many stalls that line the way to the church. Another tradition is that young women and men seeking a mate should pluck a local herb *(la hierba de enamorar)* near the hermitage to help them in their quest. While the church of San Andrés is the center of attention for those who come for healing or to find love, we discovered even more powerful places nearby.

The Fountain of Three Spouts

Follow the path down the hill from the sanctuary and you will soon reach the Fountain of the Saint.

The fountain

Like so many things in Galicia, there are folktales associated with this oracular and healing fountain. It is said that if one drinks from each of the three spouts, makes a wish, and floats a piece of bread on the waters that flow from the fountain, the wish will come true if the bread doesn't sink. We tried it and our bread didn't sink, so surely our wishes will be granted. Incidentally, there is a sign on the fountain that warns against drinking the water, but perhaps that's just a bureaucratic precaution.

The Clootie-filled Field and Meadow below

We come now to what was for us the most powerful place in San Andrés de Teixido. The well-maintained path ends at the Fountain of the Saint, but an un-

"In the Fountain of the Saint they wash and purify. This fountain, with three spouts that maintain an inalterable flow in winter and summer, is below the sanctuary; they say that the spring originates beneath the church's high altar. The pilgrim drinks from one or all three tubes, and then fills a bottle with water to take home, as if the water were blessed. In the last ten years, they've added a ritual to the fountain, fairly common in other Gallego sanctuaries: to dampen a handkerchief in it, clean the affected body part with it, and leave it there—in this case tied to a tree [or fence]." Xosé Ramón Mariño Ferro. *Santuarios Mágicos de Galicia*. Pontevedra: Colección Andaina, 2003, p. 19 (translation by Elyn Aviva).

92

The clootie-filled field

marked trail con-
tinues down the
hill. First you come
to a field where
clootie cloths are
tied to wires and
trees. Clootie cloths
are small (usu-
ally white) rags or
cloths that are as-
sociated with healing and prayer. There is a belief in
many Celtic nations that if one washes an affected
body part with water from a holy spring and ties the
cloth to a tree near the well, healing may ensue. The
clootie-filled field below the fountain is clearly a Gali-
cian version of this practice.

Continue down the path through the field and climb
down the short ladder to the meadow below. You will
find yourself in an open meadow with trees on either
side. The path leads to a stone wall; climb down the
wall to another meadow. The path ends at a row of
bushes and the edge
of the cliffs. On ei-
ther side are groves
of trees. From here
you can see some
of the highest cliffs
(over 2,000 feet) in
Europe. The view of
the Costa de Morte
(Coast of Death) is
breathtaking.

"It looked as if the clootie-cloth tradition at San Andrés had existed for
centuries—but I later learned that it's
only 10 years old. That's a reminder that
not all 'since time immemorial' rituals
are such. In fact, there are a number of
anthropological studies on the reinven-
tion of tradition. Perhaps someone came
back from a visit to Ireland or Cornwall
(both Celtic nations) and decided to rep-
licate the ritual. People asked me what
they were and I said 'prayers.' Maybe I've
started a *new* ritual." (Elyn, wearing her
anthropologist hat)

The natural forces we experienced in the center of this meadow were extremely strong. They result from underground faults, underground water sources, and the ambiance of the site. There is a powerful energy vortex near the center of the field, and a dowsing rod held up at that point will rotate quite rapidly. Find a

View from the lower field

comfortable boulder—perhaps one nearly hidden in the trees—and meditate while the sea smashes against the cliffs below and the breeze ruffles the trees. . . .

You are likely to have this powerful place mostly to yourself. The vast majority of visitors to San Andrés de Teixido stop at the hermitage. A few venture down to the fountain, fewer still to the "clootie field," and almost no one reaches the meadow below.

Other Things to Do

The resort town of Cedeira has amazing seafood (they farm mussels in the bay) and a beautiful beach. It is a pleasant place to stay while exploring the area. Cedeira is only seven miles from San Andrés de Teixido. You could walk to the shrine from there if you are so inclined. Inquire at the tourist office for directions.

(See walking map: http://pilgrim.peterrobins.co.uk/
routes/details/teixido.html)

Getting There

San Andrés de Teixido is in an isolated corner of
Galicia and is reached by car or bus. (One possibility:
http://tours.hotel.com.au/?m=tour&name=High-
Estuaries-and-Coast-of-Lugo-_-Cedeira-San-An-
dres-de-Teixido-Viveiro-Chavin&id=32536)   From
Cedeira take the AC-2204 past As Pontigas and Par-

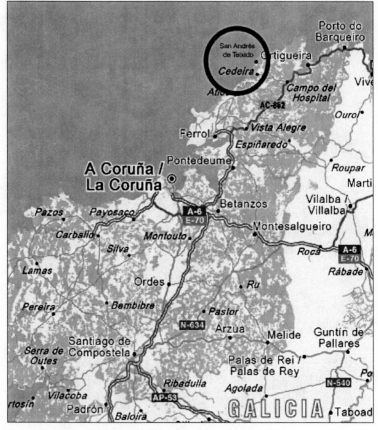

Area map

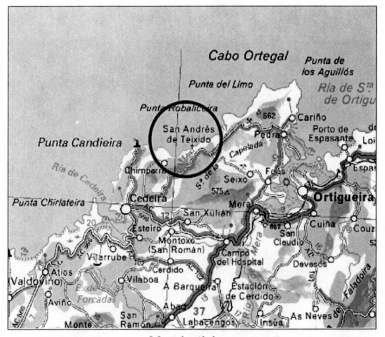

More detailed map

diñeira directly to San Andrés. This road has many steep hills and an amazing overlook at the top, but it is the most direct route to the shrine. Small signposts indicate the way to "San Andrés." Before reaching San Andrés you'll come to a TV repeater and a parking lot on the left. Here you will find part of the original pilgrims' foot trail to San Andrés. If you follow it you will come to a *milladoiro*. Drive on and you will pass a picnic area on the left with an impressive *mirador* (scenic overlook). You can also approach San Andrés de Teixido from the east. That route is slightly less twisting. A detailed road map is highly recommended for driving in Galicia as is a GPS.

Elyn Aviva

Sun on the water at Fisterre

Cabo Fisterre and Costa da Morte, A Coruña Province, Galicia

The End of the Earth. The farthest-west piece of land in Spain. Place of the setting sun, of sunken legendary lands (perhaps Atlantis lies deep beneath the seas?), of the Celtic Isle of the Dead where souls go, escorted by an owl, a spirit guide, a psychopomp.... Fisterre: the "más allá" in geography and metaphysics. The End of the Earth and the Coast of Death—not just because of the numerous ships that have wrecked themselves against its rocky cliffs.

We climbed the oversized stone steps (did giants walk here once?) to the top of the hill and waited for the sun to sink beneath the waters. For years the Church resisted the call of Fisterre, urging faithful pilgrims to end their journey at Santiago, the only acceptable goal of their Camino. But recently the Church has acknowledged the irresistible pull of the End of the Earth. "Go," the priests now say, "And watch the sun set. Contemplate the death and resurrection of Christ." Whatever one may think of that, at least we can all agree the sun will rise again tomorrow. (Elyn)

Being at the edge of the unknown has always fascinated humans. Cabo Fisterre (Finisterra in Castilian Spanish) has evoked that mystery for travelers and pilgrims for millennia. Just imagine what you would feel, looking at the Atlantic Ocean, if you believed that the world really *did* end somewhere beyond the horizon! Barren granite cliffs jutting out into the sea, the sun setting over the Atlantic Ocean, the water churning and boiling below, mists rising—it is the stuff of fantasy and legend. And legends there are.

98

Elyn at Cabo Fisterre,
lighthouse in the background

There is, of course, the ancient Celtic belief in a "Land Beyond" where souls go at death. And where might this be but somewhere off the rugged Coast of Death at Fisterre, literally the End of the Earth? Here, at the ultimate end of the Camino de Santiago (also known as the Milky Way), those beliefs are reinforced by seeing the Milky Way disappear into the ocean. Some say that every star in the Milky Way is an ascended soul and that one can see the souls returning to the *Más Allá* (the "Great Beyond") at Fisterre.

Endings and beginnings—all are there at Fisterre. Another belief, long held in Galicia, is that couples who are barren could conceive a child by sleeping on St. William's Stone (A Pedra de San Guillerme), an anthropomorphic, tomb-shaped stone near Fisterre. This stone is said to be an *ara solis* or "altar to the sun" where the Celts worshiped. This stone (perhaps a fallen menhir) was considered sacred then—and, in its

A Celt is . . . "a member of an early Indo-European people who from the second millennium BCE to the first century BCE spread over much of Europe. Their tribes and groups eventually ranged from the British Isles and northern Spain to as far east as Transylvania, the Black Sea coasts, and Galatia in Anatolia and were in part absorbed into the Roman Empire as Britons, Gauls, Boii, Galatians, and Celtiberians. Linguistically they survive in the modern Celtic speakers of Ireland, Highland Scotland, the Isle of Man, Wales, and Brittany." *Encyclopaedia Britannica Online.*

Sunset at Fisterre

Elyn Aviva

Christianized form, it still is.

The Church authorities have tried mightily to squelch pagan customs and beliefs, turning Celtic priestesses into hags and witches and applying a Christian vernier to folk customs and beliefs. (Note how the *ara solis* became St. William's Stone.) Nevertheless, in Galicia the old ways still lurk just beneath the surface. Here you will find figures of witches *(meigas)* and owls (guides for souls in the afterlife) in shop windows everywhere. Far from dying out, the old ways have simply morphed into tourist souvenirs.

The Camino de Santiago has long been conflated with the Milky Way in the heavens. This is likely due to the general east-west track of both the road and Milky Way. The Milky Way is spoken of as the Camino in the sky, and the road

"The *Santa Compaña, Rolda,* or *Estadea* as it is known in Fisterra, is still believed to appear at night bearing a coffin to the door of the one who is destined to die... The credulity and strong sense of fantasy that the inhabitants of Fisterra have, made the region a fertile environment for this ancient belief, which has passed down through the generations, and the people, accustomed to tales of the *Santa Compaña,* have come to regard it as a reality. For those who have lived with them since infancy, myths sometimes take on the semblance of truth and form part of their interior world, creating a vision of the environment which is closer to that of their ancestors than to that of our own times." Fernando Alonso Romero. *O Camiño de Fisterra.* Editións Xerais de Galicia, 1993, p. 107-108.

100

to Compostela is called the Milky Way brought down to the earth. Thus it is natural to see Fisterre as the end of the Camino: it is the place where the Milky Way and the setting sun sink into the sea.

After sunset

Some have related the Camino to a series of constellations that lie on or near the Milky Way. These constellations form a progression called the "Camino of the Stars." This is a modern addition to the inner teachings that have always swirled around the Camino.

"It is true, that the pathway in the sky, because it is filled with stars was called by the pagans The Milky Way, commonly known as the Way of St. James. And it happens that a tired laborer, coming to his humble home from the fields, one summer night, finds that his wife, wishing to flatter him, has put their bed out in the yard, in the fresh air; but he, raising his eyes heavenwards and seeing above the Way of St. James, spoke to his wife thus saying: 'Have you not noticed where you have put the bed? Do you want the staff or gourd of a pilgrim passing overhead to, perchance, fall upon us and break our heads?' And shuddering at such a thing, the couple being more frightened than ashamed, took their bed indoors." Tirso de Molina (1571-1648). quoted in L. Vázquez de Parga, et. al. *La Peregrinaciones a Santiago de Compostela.* Madrid, 1949, pp. 532-534.

Although the Church has discouraged it, pilgrims have begun going on to Fisterre from Santiago—a movement as unstoppable as the setting of the sun. In recent years pilgrims who continue on to Fisterre have taken to burning their clothes on the beach and swimming in the icy waters of the Atlantic. Many believe that burning their clothes is an ancient custom, but it is not. Medieval pilgrims would not have had more than one set of clothing, and many believed their pilgrim's gear had been embued with power and sacredness. Rather than destroy the clothes, they wanted to be buried in them.

"The Camino of the Stars"

According to Ferran Blasco, "The Camino de las Estrellas is not about tourism: it's about profound personal transformation, an inner pilgrimage of light through the central channel of individual consciousness towards recognizing and merging with universal consciousness. Through the practice of presence in its many forms, deeper layers will be revealed, including:

• The physical camino on Earth has a cosmic aspect, which is the pilgrimage through the Milky Way as the River of Wisdom towards enlightenment and transcendence.

• During this process, the changes in personal consciousness that take place along El Camino are related to a sequence of constellations.

• The ruling constellation is Canis Major and the star Sirius, which represents the Mother Goddess.

• The evolution in this River of Wisdom starts with setting the intention in the area of Scorpio and finishes with transcendence, reaching Sirius.

• This is so because consciousness is light and therefore, when through the process of being in pilgrimage one is open to the sacred (higher energies), individual consciousness is more easily transformed by the energies that these constellations emit.

• The actual constellations are not an external object but a pointer to dimensions of being that exist within the pilgrim. Walking the path activates them so that the changes can manifest."

The Fisterre region is known as "the Coast of Death" (Costa da Morte) and not just because of Celtic belief in the passage of souls over the sea to the lands in the far west. This coast has been

The Camino de Santiago is constantly changing. Burning one's clothes is another example of an invented tradition (see p. 92). It's not surprising that modern pilgrims want to perform a final ritual act or gesture that recognizes their personal transformation. The bar at the lighthouse even provides a receptacle to burn clothing—or anything else you want. Just don't make the mistake of thinking this is "traditional."

the site of many maritime disasters, including the sinking of the HMS Captain in 1870, which resulted in the loss of over 500 lives. In recent years the Costa da Morte has also been the scene of several oil spills.

The impact of the Atlantic ocean beating on granite cliffs creates an energy that is palpable to anyone who visits Cabo Fisterre. Be sure to wear layers of clothing and carry rain gear because the weather is subject to frequent changes. On our last visit we were buffeted by high winds and cold rain that drove us from the observation area on the hill into the bar near the

lighthouse. Even though we were not able to experience the fabled sunset over the Atlantic, we could still feel the elemental power of the place.

Other Things to Do

In Noia the Romanesque church of Santa María a Nova is filled with intriguing tombstones, and the church itself

Tombstone in Santa María a Nova in Noia

Elyn Aviva

Mary's stone boat in Muxía

has a delicate, sweet energy, if you give it time to unfold. (The first time Elyn went there, however, she couldn't wait to leave!) Padrón has a stone that is supposedly the mooring post for the stone boat that carried Santiago to Iberia. The stone is probably a menhir that has been incorporated into the altar. Muxía, on the other hand, has the famous Sanctuario de Nuestra Señora de la Barca, where you can see the stone boat that the Virgin Mary arrived in from Palestine. It's a huge boulder with an opening you can crawl under.

Getting There

Pilgrims walk to Cabo Fisterre but we will describe driving by car from Santiago. Outside of Santiago find AC-543 to Noia. At Noia follow the coast road (AC-550) to Cee, where you turn right on AC-552. At Toba continue on AC-445 to the village of Fisterra. This is not yet your destination. Find the AC-4408/ Calle del Alcalde Fernández toward Cabo Finisterre. This road ends in a parking lot near the lighthouse and bar. Just before this parking lot is a small road to the right. Soon the road splits; take the one on the left, leading to a parking area. Climb the steep hill with the giant steps that Elyn described earlier. At the top you'll have a spectacular view of the sea and the lighthouse. There is a simple hostal/posada connected to the bar where you can stay if you choose to spend

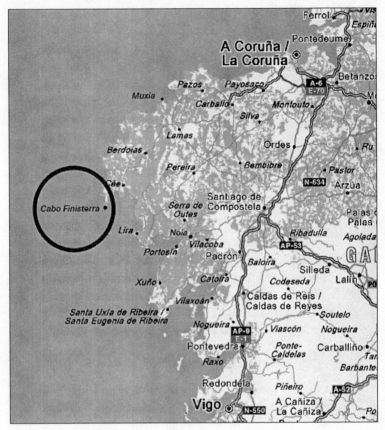

Area map

the night. You will definitely want to watch the sun set into the sea.

An alternative is to take a bus. Busses from Santiago de Compostela or A Coruña run several times per day, but you will need to walk the final two miles up to the lighthouse or take a taxi. (http://www.tripadvisor.com/Tourism-g675376-Cape_Finisterre_Galicia-Vacations.html)

Afterword

We hope you have enjoyed reading about these powerful places on the Caminos de Santiago and will visit some of them, either on foot or by car. They are quite diverse in location, spreading across Spain from east to west, and in content: a powerful Black Virgin, a hidden valley in the Pyrenees, the replica of the Grail in a thousand-year-old church, a mysterious Templar hermitage, the End of the World.

Our unifying theme has been the Caminos de Santiago, that fascinating web of trails and byways that lead, eventually, to Santiago de Compostela—and beyond. Some say the Camino de Santiago is an ancient initiatic path, perhaps followed by Druids after they completed their training near Chartres in France. Others say it was a trail followed by the Atlantians, traveling to Cabo Fisterre to contemplate the vast ocean into which their island nation sank. Some say . . . but never mind. Magic and mystery are alive throughout Spain, and the number of powerful places is enormous. We have chosen but a few.

Glossary

alchemy A type of science that alchemists used in the Middle Ages to try to change ordinary metals into gold. Also refers to a coded system of personal, spiritual transformation.

apse A curved area at the end of a church, often the location of the altar.

ashlar A squared building stone cut more or less true on all faces adjacent to those of other stones so as to permit very thin mortar joints.

barrow See tumulus.

basilica An early Christian or medieval church of the type built especially in Italy, characterized by a plan including a nave, two or four side aisles, a semicircular apse, a narthex, and often other features.

BCE Before the Common Era (replaces BC, which stood for Before Christ).

blind spring Underground water feature that has not broken through to the surface.

boss An ornamental, knoblike projection, such as a carved keystone at the intersection of arches in the vaulted ceiling of a church.

Bronze Age An age that began with metalworking, specifically the smelting of copper and tin to make bronze. The Bronze Age in Spain lasted from 2200 – 750 BCE.

capital The top part of a pillar or column, often carved.

CE Common Era (replaces AD, which means *Anno Domini*—in the year of the Lord).

Celt A nineteenth-century term used to describe any of the European peoples who spoke, or speak, a Celtic language. The term is also used in a wider sense to describe the modern descendants of those peoples, notably those who participate in a Celtic culture. A member of a group of Indo-Europeans found in Germany and France in the Second Millennium BCE (see p. 98).

chakra One of seven energy centers in the human body according to Eastern philosophy.

choir The part of a church used by a company of singers or where the priests or monks sit to pray and chant.

cloister A covered walk, especially in a religious institution, having an open arcade or colonnade usually opening onto a courtyard.

clootie cloth A strip or piece of cloth, a rag or item of clothing left at a sacred well as an offering or prayer.

conglomerate A rock consisting of pebbles or the like embedded in a finer cementing material.

crypt A subterranean chamber or vault, especially one beneath the main floor of a church.

disentailment A set of decrees from 1835-1837 that resulted in the expropriation and privatization of monastic properties in Spain.

dolmen A type of single-chamber megalithic construction, usually consisting of three or more upright stones supporting a large flat horizontal capstone. Most date from the early Neolithic period. Dolmens were usually covered with earth or small stones to form a barrow or tumulus, though in many cases that covering has weathered away.

dowse To search for underground supplies of water, metal, etc., by using a divining rod.

Druid A member of the priestly learned class in Gaul, and perhaps in Celtic culture more generally, during the final centuries BCE. They were suppressed by the Roman government from the 1st century CE and disappeared from the written record by the 2nd century, although there may have been later survivals in Britain and Ireland.

ex voto A painting or other object (or wax or metal replicas of a body part) left as an offering in fulfillment of a vow or in gratitude, as for recovery from an illness or injury.

Gothic A style of architecture, originating in France in the middle of the 12th century and existing in the western half of Europe through the middle of the 16th century, characterized by the use of the pointed arch and the ribbed vault, by the use of fine woodwork and stonework, by a progressive lightening of structure, and by the use of such features as flying buttresses.

hermitage A place where one can live in seclusion; a retreat; a kind of small church.

horseshoe arch A characteristic style of arch in Mudéjar style.

Más Allá The Great Beyond.

megalith A large stone which has been used to construct a structure or monument, either alone or together with other stones. Megalithic means structures made of such large stones, utilizing an interlocking system without the use of mortar or cement.

menhir An upright monumental stone standing either alone or with others, as in an alignment.

mihrab A niche in the wall of a mosque or a room in the mosque that indicates the direction of Mecca.

milagro A painting or other object left as an offering in fulfillment of a vow or in gratitude, as for recovery from an illness or injury. Spanish word meaning "miracle."

milladoiro A pile of rocks, often brought one by one by pilgrims en route to a shrine.

mosque A Muslim house of worship with at least one minaret, a tall, slender tower with balconies, used for calling the faithful to prayer.

Mudéjar A style of Spanish architecture of the 13th to the 16th century, combining Moorish and Gothic elements, including horseshoe arches. Mudéjars were Muslims living in Spanish territories under Christian occupation.

narthex A portico or lobby of an early Christian or Byzantine church or basilica, originally separated from the nave by a railing or screen.

nave The central part of a church, extending from the narthex to the apse and flanked by aisles.

Neolithic A period in the development of human technology, beginning about 9500 BCE in the Middle East, that is traditionally considered the last part of the Stone Age. The Neolithic begins with the rise of farming, which produced the ""Neolithic Revolution," and ends when metal tools became widespread in the Copper Age or Bronze Age or developed directly into the Iron Age, depending on geographical region. The Neolithic is not a specific chronological period, but rather a suite of behavioural and cultural characteristics, including the use of wild and domestic crops and the use of domesticated animals.

omphalos The name of the rounded stone in the shrine at Delphi, regarded by the ancients as the center of the world. A sacred center.

oratory A place for prayer, such as a small private chapel.

passage tomb A megalithic site that often, but *not always* contains bones, usually dating to the Neolithic. Some variants have simple single chambers, while others have sub-chambers leading off from the main chamber. They are ritual ceremonial centers characterised by a long covered entryway.

pentangle A five-pointed, star-shaped figure made by extending the sides of a regular pentagon until they meet.

petroglyph A carving or line drawing on rock, especially one made by prehistoric people.

presbytery The section of a church reserved for the clergy.

retablo An altarpiece in a church.

Romanesque A style of European church architecture containing both Roman and Byzantine elements, prevalent especially in the 11th and 12th centuries and characterized by massive walls, round arches, and relatively simple ornamentation.

sarcophagus A stone coffin, often inscribed or decorated with sculpture.

scriptorium A room in a monastery set aside for the copying, writing, or illuminating of manuscripts and records.

Shangri La An imaginary paradise on earth, esp. a remote and exotic utopia.

Templar A member of a religious military order, the Poor Knights of the Temple of Solomon (see p. 64), founded by Crusaders in Jerusalem about 1118 and suppressed in 1312.

"thin place" A place (in nature or in a human construction) where the veil between this world and other realms (fairy, the Other World, etc.) is thin and passage between our normal consensual reality and a different kind of reality is more easily accomplished.

tumulus A mound of earth and stones raised over a grave or graves. Tumuli are also known as barrows, burial mounds, *Hügelgrab* or *kurgans*, and can be found throughout much of the world.

Visigoth A member of the western Goths that invaded the Roman Empire in the 4th century CE and settled in France and Spain, establishing a monarchy that lasted until the early 8th century (see p. 73).

Visigothic (art style) A style of art and architecture heavily influenced by Roman, Byzantine, and North African art—especially the horseshoe arch (see p. 83).

vortex A funnel shape created by a whirling fluid or by the motion of spiraling energy. In dowsing, a vortex is spiraling subtle energy.

Bibliography

(This list includes books cited in this guidebook as well as books of interest)

Alarcón H., Rafael. *A la sombra de los Templarios*. In the series "Colección Enigmas del Cristianismo." Barcelona: Martinez Roca, 1986.

Almazan de Gracia, Ángel, ed. *Esoterismo Templario –Santo Alto Rey— Albendiego (Guadalajara) y San Bartolo en el Cañón del Río Lobos (Soria)*. 2nd edition. Soria: Sotabur SL, 2005.

Arias Páramo, Lorenzo. *The Pre-Romanesque in Asturias – The Art of the Asturian Monarchy*. Gijón (Asturias): Ediciones Trea, 2nd edition and 1st English edition, 1999.

Aviva, Elyn. *Following the Milky Way: A Pilgrimage on the Camino de Santiago*. 2nd Edition. Santa Fe: Pilgrims Process, Inc., 2002.

———. *Dead End on the Camino*. Santa Fe: Pilgrims Process, Inc., 2002.

———. *The Journey: A Novel of Pilgrimage and Spiritual Quest*. Santa Fe: Pilgrims Process, Inc., 2004.

———. *Walking Through Cancer: A Pilgrimage of Gratitude on the Way of St. James*. Santa Fe: Pilgrims Process, Inc., 2009.

Begg, Ean. *The Cult of the Black Virgin*. Revised and expanded edition. London: Arkana – Penguin Books, 1996.

Boix, Maur M. *What is Montserrat*. Montserrat: Publicacions de l'Abadia de Montserrat, 1998.

Devereux, Paul. *Earth Memory: Sacred Sites—Doorways into Earth's Mysteries*. St. Paul, MN: Llewellyn Publications, 1992.

———. *Places of Power: Secret Energies at Ancient Sites: A Guide to Observed or Measured Phenomena*. London: Blandford, 1990.

——— *The Sacred Place: The Ancient Origin of Holy and Mystical Sites*. London: Cassel & Co., 2000.

114

Díez Tejón, Luis. *Prerrománico y Románico en Asturias.* 3rd edition. León: Ediciones Lancia, 2008.

Escolano Benito, Agustín. *San Baudelio de Berlanga – Guía y Complementarios.* New edition. In the series, "Rutas de la Memoria." Necodisne Ediciones, 2003.

Furlong, David. *Working with Earth Energies: How to Tap into the Healing Powers of the Natural World.* London: Judy Piatkus (Publishers) Ltd, 2003.

Heselton, Philip. *Earth Mysteries.* Shaftsbury, Dorset: Element Books Ltd, 1995.

Lacarra Ducay, María del Carmen. *The Monastery of Leyre.* Editur. s/d.

Lapeña Paúl, Ana Isabel. *San Juan de la Peña – A historical and artistic guide.* Diputación General de Aragón, Departamento de Cultura y Educación, 1987.

Lapunzina, Alejandro. *Architecture of Spain.* In the series, "Reference Guides to National Architecture." Westport, CT: Greenwood Press, 2005.

Lonegren, Sig. *Spiritual Dowsing.* Glastonbury: Gothic Image Publications, 1996.

Mariño Ferro, Xosé Ramón. *Sanctuarios mágicos de Galicia.* Vigo (Ponferrada): Edicións Nigratrea, 2003.

Matthews, John. *The Elements of the Grail Tradition.* Rockport, MA: Element Books, 1991.

Pennick, Nigel. *Celtic Sacred Landscapes.* New York: Thames & Hudson Inc., 1996.

Petzold, Andreas. *Romanesque Art.* Upper Saddle River, NJ: Prentice Hall, 1995.

Pogacnik, Marko. *Sacred Geography: Geomancy: Co-Creating the Earth Cosmos.* Great Barrington, MA: Lindisfarne Books, 2007.

Romero, Fernando Alonso. *O Camiño de Fisterra.* (In Gallego, Spanish, and English.) Edicións Xerais de Galicia, 1993.

Sánchez Dragó, Fernando. *Historia mágica del Camino de Santiago.* 3rd edition. Barcelona: Planeta, 1999.

Soler i Canals, Fr Josep. *All Montserrat.* Editorial Fisa Escudo de Oro, s/d.

The Roads to Santiago de Compostela. Text written with collaboration of Julie Roux; help and advice of Centro Estudios Camino Santiago – Sahagún, and Humbert Jacomet. "In Situ" series. Vic-en-Bigorre Cedex, France: MSM, 2007.

Tilly, C. "Art, Architecture, Landscape." In *Landscape: Politics and Perspectives,* edited by Barbara Bender. Providence/Oxford: Berg Publishers, 1994.

Wallace-Murphy, Tim. *Cracking the Symbol Code: Revealing the Secret Heretical Messages within Church and Renaissance Art.* London: Watkins Publishing, 2005.

LaVergne, TN USA
30 December 2010
210612LV00001B/39/P